Mobility in Smart Cities-
Young India's Aspirations

Mobility in Smart Cities- Young India's Aspirations

PROF. (DR.) NIRUPAMA PRAKASH
Director, Amity Institute of Social Sciences,
Amity University Sector 125, Noida, Uttar Pradesh 201303, India.

Ms. RASHMI KAPOOR
Research Associate,
Swinburne University of Technology, Hawthorn VIC 3122, Australia.

PROF. (DR.) AJAY KAPOOR
Prof Vice-Chancellor (Research Sarawak),
Swinburne University of Technology, Hawthorn VIC 3122, Australia.

Mr. YASHPAL MALIK
Research Associate, Amity Institute of Social Sciences,
Amity University Sector 125, Noida, Uttar Pradesh 201303, India.

Mr. SATYA PRAKASH GARADA
Project Fellow, Amity Institute of Social Sciences,
Amity University Sector 125, Noida, Uttar Pradesh 201303, India.

ZORBA BOOKS

ZORBA BOOKS

Publishing in India by Zorba Books, 2019
Website: www.zorbabooks.com
Email: info@zorbabooks.com

SUHREC Number: 2018/100 'Mobility in Smart Cities: Young India's Aspirations'

Print Book ISBN: 978-93-88497-19-0
eBook: 978-93-88497-26-8

Zorba Books Pvt. Ltd.(opc)
Gurgaon, INDIA

Contents

Abbreviation

₹	Indian Rupees
10 lakh	1 million
BRT	Bus Rapid Transport
CCTV	Closed–Circuit Television
CNG	Compressed Natural Gas
Crore	1,00,00,000 (10 million)
DJB	Delhi Jal Board
DMRC	Delhi Metro Rail Corporation
DTC	Delhi Transport Corporation
EV	Electric Vehicle (Here Used For Full Battery Electric Vehicle, Often Called BEV)
GoI	Government of India
GPS	Global Positioning System
ICT	Information and Communications Technology
Lakh	1,00,000 (.1 million)
LMRC	Lucknow Metro Rail Corporation
MCD	Municipal Corporation of Delhi
MoUHA	Ministry of Housing and Urban Affairs
NCR	National Capital Region
NH	National Highway
OBC	Other Backward Classes
PPP	Public Private Partnership
PWD	Public Works Department
RTV	Rapid Transit Vehicle
SUHREC	Swinburne University Human Research Ethics Committee

ToI	Times of India
ULBs	Urban Local Bodies
UNDP	United Nations Development Programme
UPSRTC	Uttar Pradesh State Road Transport Corporation
USD	US Dollar

Preface

This book is a detailed exploratory research study based on the project titled "Mobility in Smart Cities-Young India's Aspirations" and data has been collected during June 2018 to Sep 2018 to understand perceptions of the urban youth regarding mobility in smart cities in Delhi-NCR (Delhi, Gurugram, Noida) and Lucknow. The data was analyzed in the backdrop of socio-economic variables such as gender, income and education. This collaborative work by researchers from Amity Institute of Social Sciences, Amity University, Noida, India and from Swinburne University of Technology, Hawthorn, Australia led to this book highlighting usage of transport, time and money spent on transport, problems faced by them and their preferences for Smart Cities vision now and for future.

Policy makers, real estate companies, students, researchers will find answers to the questions they are asking while getting ready for the era of smart transport. They will come to know from this book about the expectations of youth from smart cities in the coming years and how society can help the civic bodies in prioritizing the implementations of schemes effectively and efficiently.

Acknowledgements

The authors express their gratitude to Dr. Ashok K. Chauhan, Hon'ble Founder President, Amity Education Group for constant encouragement in undertaking innovative research. The authors are indebted to Hon'ble Chancellor Amity University, Uttar Pradesh, Dr. Atul Chauhan for showing us the path to work towards academic excellence. We acknowledge with respect Prof. (Dr.) Balvinder Shukla, Vice Chancellor, Amity University, UP for her constant support and guidance in undertaking research for societal development. We duly acknowledge Prof. Linda Kristjanson, Vice Chancellor, Swinburne University of Technology, Hawthorn, Australia for her support and encouragement in research initiatives. The authors acknowledge the financial support by Auto CRC, Melbourne, Australia for smooth conduct of the project leading to joint international publication.

Chapter 1
Introduction

Urbanization has been spreading across the world since the last couple of decades producing socio-economic, cultural and environmental transformation. India has urbanized at the annual rate of (2.47%) according to the 2010-15 estimates and likely to grow at an annual rate of (2.28%) during the 2015-20 estimates. (33.5%) of India's total population is urban (The World Factbook 2017). Every year, millions of migrants move from one place to another in search of employment opportunities, improved living conditions, better education and health facilities, better transport-related facilities, skill upgradation and entrepreneurship. Cities have always been economic and cultural poles, but recently there has been an increase in their political importance and capacity to contribute to the national Gross Domestic Product (OECD Regions at a Glance 2013). City attractiveness is a competitive factor distinguishing the better urban living areas and driving local resources, localization of research centers, large companies, cultural bodies and so on (Quality of life in cities 2013).

The speed of urbanization urges a phenomenal administrative and policy challenge and requires better coordination among all stakeholders involved in implementing innovative projects. Urban India today is varied in terms of its physical landscape with a diverse range of small and large cities spread across the country. As the urban population and wages increase, demand for each key service, for example, water, transportation, sewage treatment, low budget hotels will expand five-to-seven-fold in all the cities, regardless of size. However, if India continues to grow in the present way, the urban system is likely to gloss over an important point concerning what is key to managing a prosperous city.

Moreover, not many Indian cities have 2030 ground-breaking strategies that consider top transportation loads, prerequisites for low-wages, reasonable lodging and environmental changes. In India, the ability to execute the urban changes and tasks at the municipal and state level have been primarily lacking (Planning Commission 2012). In the year 2015, leaders from 193 countries across the world came together and created a plan called the 'Sustainable Development Goals 2030'. The area of transportation is given one of the top priorities in the 2030 strategy because it inspires local governments to transform their transport systems and mobility patterns to reduce automobile dependency and become more sustainable, low-carbon and people-centric. The leaders called for a dedicated debate on these emerging trends, new technologies, subsidies and necessary bans, including their opportunities, challenges and threats. The strategy strengthens eco-mobile solutions such as walking, cycling, public transports and their interconnectivity as the backbone of the future urban mobility (EcoMobility sessions 2017@COP23 2017).

Expanding urbanization also produces various challenges such as environmental pollution, traffic congestions, accidents, noise pollution, health-related diseases, Traffic

Management System[1] related issues and many more. This rapid growth in a short period of time puts an inevitable demand on city infrastructure and produces deteriorating living conditions. Planning also becomes difficult as better infrastructure facilities are expected from these urbanizations.

1.1 Urbanization and Transportation Challenges

Presently, all urban areas and towns of India are experiencing an acute type of transport challenge. Transport problems have increased over time and have turned out to be more complex than previously imagined as the towns develop in size. Wherever trade is important, commercial vehicles such as tempos and trucks make the problem of traffic more complicated. In different towns, narrow streets which were constructed well before motorized transport and absence of parking facilities are the key problems of congestion (Carlos 2010).

Traffic congestion on Indian roads has increased exponentially over the years. This has an adverse impact on the environment, effects productivity, increases fuel wastage, road accidents and hampers the quality of life. There are many reasons leading to traffic congestion –

1. Encroachments by private bodies on roads.
2. Unplanned road designs for larger population.
3. Lack of integrated mode of transport.
4. Minimal coordination among government departments, i.e. Public Works Department (PWD), Telecom, Electricity and many others.

---

1 Traffic Management Services integrates technology primarily to improve the flow of vehicle traffic and improve safety.

1.2 Problems with Urban Transport

The impact of the transport system on the atmosphere is significant and it contributes to approximately (20%-25%) of global emissions. Almost (95%) of the energy which is used by the transport sector in the world comes from fossil fuels (Global Greenhouse Gas Emissions Data 2017). Rapid growth of the transport sector has increased the contribution of emissions in the environment resulting in adverse living conditions for human life.

There are social costs which are linked to transport systems, which include various factors such as air pollution, noise pollution, road crashes, physical inactivity, the time taken by the family while commuting and vulnerability to fuel price increases (Squires 2012). Congestion of traffic is another factor which limits the timely delivery of various goods and services. These factors create a negative impact on those people who are planning to buy their own cars (Weisbrod and Fitzroy 2011).

Today, conventional planning of the transport system struggles to improve the mobility of human beings and related necessities. The main purpose of the transport system is to access the various functions that include work, education, goods and services, friends and family. There are many strategies[2] available in the world by which traffic congestions can be managed and simultaneously control or reduce the adverse impact on the environment and society. Communities

---

2   Traffic Demand Management strategies includes road pricing, fuel pricing, parking management and parking pricing, access management, traffic signal spacing and timing, vehicle restrictions and pedestrian improvements.

play a significant role in ensuring the sustainability of their transport system (Issa 2014).

Professor Gwailliam (2017) highlights in his report that the growth rate of traffic is much greater than the growth rate of road space. This has resulted in many problems that are prominent across urban areas. Some of the issues are as follows :-

Traffic jams and parking difficulties: The cities start facing fully packed traffic jams, especially during office hours wherever there is a population of 1 million or above.

Shortage of public transport: During the peak hours of traffic, most of the public transport is either over-utilized or under-utilized. When public transport is under-utilized, it makes the services financially unviable.

High maintenance costs: Cities that have older infrastructures struggle financially in terms of maintenance and upkeep. It becomes extremely difficult for them to upgrade the transport infrastructure which involves high costs.

Adverse impact on environment: Vehicular pollution has a serious impact on the environment in urban areas which leads to severe health issues and hampers quality of life.

Increased accidents and safety related concerns: In developing countries, the number of accidents have increased because of increased traffic. The accidents also lead to recurring delays. Increase in traffic leads to discomfort in using streets.

1.3 Traffic Congestion

Various estimates show that India is losing ₹600 billion annually because of traffic congestion and this will increase to around ₹980 billion by 2030 unless the Government of India (GoI) takes action to de-congest the roads (Joseph, Raina and Jagannathan 2015).

In reference to Delhi, various types of vehicles cause an uncontrollable chaos on the streets. Overwhelming traffic and congestion lead to blockage in the traffic system, fuel wastage, ecological contamination and loss of valuable time (Master Plan for Delhi - 2021 2010). Estimates by Center for Science and Environment (CSE) highlights that traffic congestion on the Delhi roads is increasing (7%) annually and has crossed the 10 million mark in 2007. This has resulted in a huge increase in traffic on arterial roads leading to massive accidents, heavy traffic problem and lower speed of vehicles which increases the carbon emission especially during peak hours (Banerjee 2017).

1.4 Investments in Urban Infrastructure

The Government of India is promoting Public Private Partnership (PPP) as an effective tool for bringing private sector efficiency in the creation of economic social infrastructure assets and for delivery of quality public services. The Ministry of Housing and Urban Affairs[3] (MoUHA) has envisaged creating 100 smart cities by 2022 to control the expanding urbanization and has been allotted USD 1.2 billion in the fiscal year of 2014-15 (Smart Cities 2015). The investment strategy is to be planned through the collaboration between the public and private sector participation through Public Private Partnership (PPP) and stand–alone private partners. The vision of MoUHA is "to facilitate creation of economically vibrant, inclusive, efficient and sustainable urban habitats" and the mission is "to promote cities as engines

---

3   Ministry of Housing and Urban Affairs (MoHUA), Government of India, is the apex body for formulation and administration of the rules and regulations and laws relating to the housing and urban development in India.

of economic advancement through improvement of better transportation facilities, quality of life and assured services levels" (Strategic Plan of Ministry of Urban Development for 2011-16 n.d.).

The MoUHA has announced development programs such as AMRUT[4] and Swachh Bharat Mission which covers 500 cities across the country by strengthening urban infrastructures (Improving Lives: Urban Infrastrcture 2017). The total population to be impacted is 99,486,840 (Smart Cities Mission 2017). The smart solution incorporates e-governance and citizen services, waste management, water management, energy management, urban mobility, telemedicine, tele-education and skill development centers. The Ministry has emphasized more on better transport systems which address smart parking, intelligent traffic management, integrated multimodal transport, low carbon vehicle, video surveillance inside buses using closed-circuit television (CCTV) surveillance etc. Public transit and traffic operation and management centers have been established in major cities like Delhi, Jaipur, Surat, Ahmadabad and many more (Seetharaman 2015). India is a large country and has good infrastructure like roads, railways and airports connecting all the major cities. Without clean transportation, no city can have a sustainable future. A weak transport system stifles the monetary boom and development. Green transport systems provide many monetary and social advantages in the cities, both directly and indirectly. It has a direct impact on employment, revenue value, large market in addition to time and cost upgrades.

---

4   AMRUT stands for Atal Mission for Rejuvenation and Urban Transformation launched in June 2015 to strengthen the urban infrastructure projects.

1.5 Role of Youth in Nation Building

According to the Census of India 2011, one-third of the Indian population is in the age group of 15-34 years. We are the youngest nation in the world and have the necessary resources such as huge manpower, growing education, rapid urbanization, natural resources and geography for the overall development of the country. The younger generation can best implement the policies, development works, plans and can take primary responsibility in nation building.

It has been widely recognized that the economic development of a nation is dependent on the quality of its youth. India's National Youth Policy 2012 "seeks to ensure that youth needs and concerns are mainstreamed into overall national development policies, underscoring the need for the wholesome development of the young people and optimum utilization of their potential for national development" (National Youth Policy 2012 n.d.). Understanding youth perceptions, their expectations and choices are crucial for the introduction of relevant policies and initiatives that drive the development process in the most appropriate manner.

1.6 Need for the study

Cities are sustainable for urban communities and making the city citizen-centric should be a key area of concern. Every citizen has their own priorities based on urban challenges, issues, demographics and various socio-economic dimensions. The Urban Local Bodies (ULB) must prepare the smart city plan keeping in mind the citizen's interests, needs and aspirations and involve them actively in the construction of the city. Perceptions about short term and long-term visions can help the civic bodies in prioritizing their investment plans. Projects that resolve the major issues affecting the respondents should be prioritized. The concerned authority should engage the respondents of urban areas and should have regular communication during the planning, development and implementation of smart city projects. Proper communication can help to get feedback on various dimensions including citizens' security, transportation facilities, traffic and related pollution level, education, safety, infrastructure issues, sanitation issues, job opportunities and their quality, crime rates, governance, service delivery and affordable housing among others.

1.7 Selection of cities

The research team has chosen Delhi NCR[5] (National Capital Region-Delhi, Gurugram, Noida) and Lucknow to understand the perceptions of urban youth for the upcoming transport infrastructure under smart cities. The objective of choosing the cities mentioned above is to compare the difference in perceptions among Tier-1 cities and Tier-2 cities[6]. Another reason was that all the surveyed cities are currently facing traffic congestion and pollution related issues. After inclusion in the Smart City Mission, the focus is on building more inclusive lead development by respective governments. Mobility is one of the most difficult issues in metropolitan cities and has both environmental and economic impact. All the surveyed cities have been badly affected by carbon emission due to the presence of a heavy transport system within the city. Delhi is

---

5 According to the National Capital Region Planning Board, the NCR covers the whole of NCT-Delhi and certain districts of Haryana, Uttar Pradesh and Rajasthan.

6 The classification of Indian cities is a ranking system used by the Government of India to allocate House Rent Allowance (HRA) to public servants employed in different cities in India. Cities are classified on the basis of their population into three categories – Tier 1, Tier 2 and Tier 3.

becoming one of the most populous cities in the world and the transportation facility in the current form does not adequately meet the requirements of its citizens.

1.7.1 Brief about Delhi-NCR

The National Capital Region has an area of about 53, 817 sq. km. and contributes approximately (7.1%) to the National Gross Domestic Product and is home to approximately 46 million people (Singh 2015).

Municipal Corporation

The Municipal Corporation has been involved with many duties including planning, implementing and monitoring of various development projects, providing basic facilities and services to citizens, construction of social and physical infrastructure, generating alternative ways to increase the municipal revenue, etc. The surveyed cities are covered under the following corporations –

	Delhi	**Gurgaon**	**Noida**	**Lucknow**
Name of the Municipal Corporation	New Delhi Municipal Corpora-tion, Delhi Canton-ment Board and Munic-ipal Cor-poration of Delhi	Municipal Corporation of Guru-gram	NOIDA[7] Authority	Lucknow Municipal Corpora-tion

---

7   New Okhla Industrial Development Authority (NOIDA) is a part of National Capital Region and came into administrative existence on 17th April 1976.

Transport system in Delhi–NCR

Delhi has a massive network of transport systems which are the lifeline of the city. Delhi largely relies on its public transport system. Delhi Metro Rail Corporation (DMRC) often known as Metro, is one of the most used modern means of transport in Delhi-NCR which has developed over the previous decade. The cumulative ridership of DMRC in the financial year 2016-17 crossed 1 billion passengers and became the backbone of the NCR. "The DMRC today ranks 10th in terms of ridership among the 34 top Metro systems of the world" (http://www.delhimetrorail. com 2017). On the other hand, the inhabitants of Delhi lose nearly 420 million work hours every month while traveling home through public transport due to traffic congestion during peak hours (http://www.igovernment. in 2013). Therefore, there is a strong need of putting other infrastructure projects on priority so that commuters can reply on other public transport mode like e-rickshaw, bus and shared auto.

The various public transport systems in Delhi-NCR include: Delhi Transport Corporation (DTC) auto rickshaws, bus service, cycle rickshaws, DMRC, e-rickshaws, gramin sewa[8], rapid metro in Gurugram and taxis. Other transportation facilities include inter-state bus services and private taxies which are rented for various purposes. In Delhi -NCR buses continue to be the major public transport for intra-city travel, serving about (60%) of the total commuting requirements (Dave 2016). Delhi also started the Bus Rapid Transport (BRT)

---

8   Gramin Sewa is shared auto service which operates in certain parts of Delhi and normally connected to the metro station from different locations. The vehicle normally boards around 8 to 10 commuters at a time.

system in 2008 but closed down in 2016 due to low frequency of buses, untrained drivers, limited crossing for pedestrians and slow speed of buses (Delhi BRT System –Lessons Learnt 2016). The Delhi Government is planning to build 413 km metro, 292 km of BRT and 50 km each of monorail and light rail by 2020 (Transport System in Delhi 2018).

Auto-rickshaws

In Delhi-NCR, auto-rickshaws are the most convenient means of public transportation as they are cheaper than hiring a cab or taxi. Sometimes, hiring an auto in Delhi gets highly dubious as auto drivers usually do not agree to the standard meter charges.

Bus

DTC has a fleet of Air Conditioned (AC) and Non-Air-Conditioned buses to phase out the traditional buses. DTC also has private buses which run in the PPP mode[9] to support the public transport system (Saxena 2011). The GPS[10] system in the DTC buses and bus station is going to be integrated to convey the right information about bus arrivals. This will help the commuters save time by giving the right information about arrival timings and guide them for the preferred route which can lead to their destination in the shortest possible time (Roy 2017).

---

9   Gross Cost Model has been adopted for the private buses in Delhi so they do not compete with each other.
10 Global Positioning System (GPS) is a device that gives commuter an accurate location in the names of longitude and latitude anywhere and anytime of any person or vehicle.

Taxis

Despite the fact that taxis and cabs are easily accessible, they are not a major part of the transport system in Delhi. The taxis are owned by private operators and permitted by State Transport Department. Now, a days taxis are operating through app based platforms, such as Ola and Uber, in Delhi-NCR and becoming the preferred mode of private transport.

Rickshaws (cycle and electric)

For a few kilometers of travel within the city, rickshaw is the best option for travel. The rickshaws (cycle rickshaw and electric-rickshaw) are effortlessly accessible all through the city and known for being affordable and ecologically friendly. There are more than 1 lakh[11] e-rickshaws and around 8 lakh cycle rickshaws available in Delhi-NCR as on November 2017 (Goswami 2017).

Other Public Transportation

Majority of commuters in the National Capital depend on other public transport like metro feeder[12], auto-rickshaw, gramin sewa and Rapid Transit Vehicle (RTV)[13] for daily traveling within different parts of the city. Buses continue to be the major means of transport and cover almost all the suburban areas of the city.

1.7.2 Brief about Lucknow

Lucknow is one of the developed urban cities of Uttar Pradesh and is linked with the rest of the country through roadways,

---

11 1 lakh is equal to 0.1 million.
12 Metro feeders are connected to metro stations and can carry 18-20 passengers at a time.
13 RTV is a bus which carries around 18-20 passengers at a time.

airways and railways. In terms of connectivity within the city, Lucknow has only 6 buses per lakh of population making the public transport system inadequate (BBA|mantra, 2018). It is much lower than the benchmark figure which is between 70 buses to 80 buses per lakh in urban areas. With limited availability of bus transport and heavy dependence on private transport, Lucknow became the most polluted city in India in November 2017 with the Air Quality Index[14] (AQI) of 484. Above AQI 500, cities are declared as a public health hazard due to spreading of diseases like chronic obstructive pulmonary disease, respiratory infection, lung cancer etc. It becomes critical to study the perceptions of youth for various transportation facilities available to them to commute and understand their views on various other important issues such as greenery and cleanliness, infrastructure, sewerage, crime rates, pollution level, governance and many others.

Transport system in Lucknow

The major public transport system in the city includes taxis, auto rickshaws, city buses, CNG buses, cycles and electric rickshaws. The city transport system is operated by Lucknow Mahanagar Parivahan Sewa which is a part of Uttar Pradesh State Road Transport Corporation (UPSRTC).

Auto Rickshaws and Taxis

Auto rickshaws are also major sources of mobility in Lucknow. These rickshaws run across the city and are well connected to different locations. They are capable of accommodating around

---

14 The National Air Quality Index (AQI) is measured by Central Pollution Control Board with State Pollution Control Boards. There are 6 categories of AQI, i.e. Good (0–50), Satisfactory (51-100), Moderately polluted (101–200), Poor (201–300), Very poor (301–400), Severe (401–500).

four people per trip. Auto rickshaws are mostly used on a sharing basis but they can also be reserved. There are two types of taxis available in the city, prepaid taxis and 24/7 radio taxis. Taxis are available through travel agents or on personal call basis. These taxis are operated by private agents and organizations.

Buses

Local bus services are the major means of transport in the city and are connected to major cities in the state. These buses are managed by the state government transportation departments. The city operates around 300 CNG buses out of the total fleet of 9500. The city is connected with around 35 bus routes covering different parts of the city. Lucknow Mahanagar Parivahan Sewa or Lucknow city transport services, as it is prevalently known, was built up to take into account the increasing requirements of Lucknow City. Lucknow Mahanagar Parivahan Sewa runs a large number of A/C and Non-A/C, low and semi low floor buses. Mini buses[15] are small in size and normally operate on smaller routes. These bus services only have basic facilities in terms of comfort and security. Other services are also available like other tourist transport buses operated by travel agents for tourists to travel around the city.

E-Rickshaws

In Lucknow, the estimated the number of registered and non-registered e-rickshaws is put at more than 1.5 lakh and one of the major sources of travel for main and feeder routes. Uttar Pradesh transport department is planning to ban these battery-driven vehicles on the main routes and have them

---

15 Mini buses have a seating capacity of 25 to 30 passengers and are often covers the short travel, i.e. 10-15 kms in a single side trip.

operate only on feeder routes that are without other modes of public transport (Parashar 2018).

Lucknow Metro Rail Corporation (LMRC)

The metro service was started in Lucknow on 5th September 2017. Metro train has been designed to accommodate about 1100 commuters at a time. The train coaches have multiple safety features such as emergency communication; facilities for differently-abled passengers including dedicated wheel chair spaces and braille stickers for the visually handicapped (Lucknow Metro Rail Corporation). The 1st phase was inaugurated on 5th September 2017 from Charbagh Railway Station to Transport Nagar. As of now, with 8 operational metro stations, the LMRC provides limited connectivity to the commuters of Lucknow.

1.8 Study Objectives

This study was conducted to understand the perceptions of urban youth related to transport modes available to them. The study also highlights several key issues in the transport system used by the urban youth and elements of smart cities that demand attention with regard to meeting future demands and prioritizing the implementations of schemes effectively and efficiently.

The objectives of the study are:
- To study the current usage of transport, time spent, money spent, problems faced.
- To identify the priorities that require immediate attention and issues that need to be addressed within a decade.
- To understand existing challenges in the surveyed cities and perceived improvement areas for the next 5 years.
- To understand the perceptions of transport system available for mobility of goods and removal of waste material.

1.9 Methodology

The study was exploratory and analytical in nature. The target population for the study was between the age group of 18-25 years who are enrolled in undergraduate and postgraduate programmes in universities and those who have completed their graduation degree and are now preparing for competitive exams.

Quota sampling[16] was used to select the respondents. A total of 2000[17] respondents were covered in the study from Delhi- NCR (Delhi, Gurugram, Noida) and Lucknow and their responses were recorded through a structured questionnaire using 4 point and 5 point Likert Scale[18] (Annexure 1). The data was collected through personal interview method and administered by the research team. Primary data was collected from June 2018 to Sep 2018. During the data digitization, it was observed that 45 questionnaires were not filled properly and hence excluded from data analysis. 1955 questionnaires were digitized completely and analyzed in Microsoft Excel to meet the objectives of the study. Frequency distributions and cross tabulations were performed.

---

16 Quota sampling is a non-probability sampling technique wherein the assembled sample has the same proportions of individuals as the entire population with respect to known characteristics, traits or focused phenomenon.

17 According to Census of India 2011, the youth population of Lucknow and Delhi NCR (Delhi, Gurgram, Noida) is approximately 1.9 Crore. Hence, each unit of sample represents the responses of approx. 10,000 respondents.

18 *Likert Scale* is a psychometric scale where questions based on this scale are normally used in a survey. It is one of the most widely used question types in a survey.

The questionnaire was broadly divided into three parts as described in the section below:

- In **Part 1** of the questionnaire, questions related to socio-demographic characteristics such as gender, age group, education level, education streams, number of family members and type of residence were included.

- In **Part 2** of the questionnaire, the focus was on mobility. The questions included how frequently they use public transports, how much time it takes them to commute to work/university, how much they pay for mobility, what kind of problems they face in transport, perceptions about services that can be improved in the near future, type of transport which is likely to be better in future smart cities, how many respondents are ready to pay premium for better services, how government policies can improve urban transport system, perceptions about automobile and green transport, how efficient is the transport system for mobility of goods and for removal of waste material.

- In **Part 3** of the questionnaire, the attempt was to understand other important issues. The questions included priorities that require immediate attention or in a decade, essence/elements which can be used in the making of a smart city, challenges faced in day-to-day lives, perceived improvement of challenges in the next five years, prioritization of features in making an existing city a smart city, respondents' view on whether there will be improvement in the challenges faced.

In the next chapter, socio-demographic characteristics such as gender, education level, education stream, number of family members, family income of the respondents will be discussed.

Chapter 2
Demography of Respondents

The study was completed in four cities namely, Delhi, Gurugram, Noida and Lucknow. The socio-economic analysis of the responses is as follows:

2.1 Gender

The study has covered 1955 respondents, out of which there were 1082 males (55%) and 873 females (45%). Figure 2.1 highlights that the percentage of male respondents is significantly more than female respondents. This is because in many of the institutions covered under the study the total number of male enrollment was more than the female enrollment.

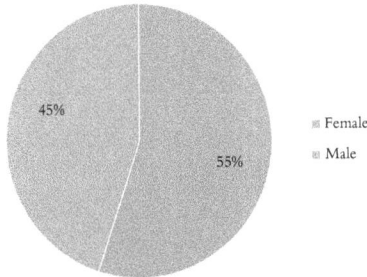

Figure 2.1: Gender

2.2 Education level of respondents

Figure 2.2 highlights the current education level of the respondents covered under the study. Total 1955 respondents' enrollment has been divided into 3 levels, i.e. undergraduates, graduates and postgraduates. The percentage of enrollment at undergraduate level is (87%) and at graduate level it is

(12%). A few respondents (1%) from postgraduate level were covered in the study.

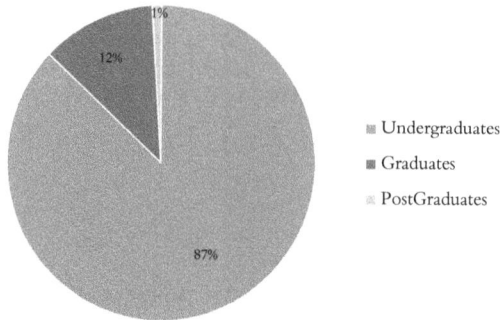

Figure 2.2: *Education Level of the Respondents*

2.3 Education Stream

Table 2.1 shows different streams of respondents covered in the study. It is visible that the highest percentage of respondents are enrolled in Management (32%), Communication has the second highest, (15%) enrollment and Engineering comes at the third place with (14%) of respondents. Likewise, the study also shows that enrollment in Arts is (13%), Social Sciences (11.8%) and Computer Science and Information Technology is (14%). The data shows that there are significant number of respondents who have opted for professional courses as opposed to Social Sciences/Arts because of the current market oriented jobs and opportunities.

Table 2.1: *Education stream enrolled in*

	N* = 1955	N%
Arts	258	13%
Communication	296	15%
Computer Science/IT	270	14%
Engineering	282	14%
Management	617	32%

	N* = 1955	**N%**
Social Science	232	12%
Total	1955	100

★N = total number of respondents covered in the study

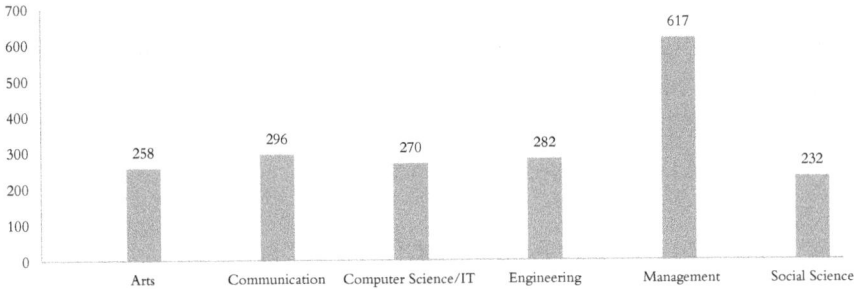

Figure 2.3: Education stream enrolled in

2.4   Number of family members

Figure 2.4 highlights that out of 1955 respondents, there are 78 (4%) families which have more than 5 members, 1505 (77 %) have 3 to 5 members and 371 (19%) families have 2 members in their family. The figure also shows that the percentage of families with 3-5 members are significantly higher than the other categories.

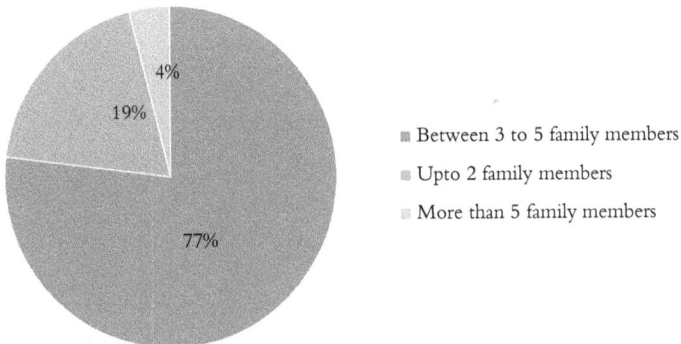

Figure 2.4: Number of family members

2.5 Family Income

Table 2.2 and Figure 2.5 highlight the number of families with different levels of income. The yearly income level range varies from less than ₹1 lakh to more than ₹12 lakh. As per the study, out of 1955 respondents (8%) of families have an annual income of less than ₹1 lakh while (18.1%) of families have an annual income between ₹1 lakh to ₹3 lakh. Most respondents (27.9%) come from families with an annual income of ₹3 lakh to ₹5 lakh and (22.1%) respondents have more than ₹12 lakh yearly income.

Table 2.2: Yearly Income of Families (In ₹)

Income group	N	N%
Less than ₹1 lakh	158	8%
₹1 lakh to ₹3 lakh	354	18%
₹3 lakh to ₹5 lakh	546	28%
₹5 lakh to ₹8 lakh	287	15%
₹8 lakh to ₹12 lakh	175	9%
> ₹12 lakh	435	22%
Total	**1955**	**100%**

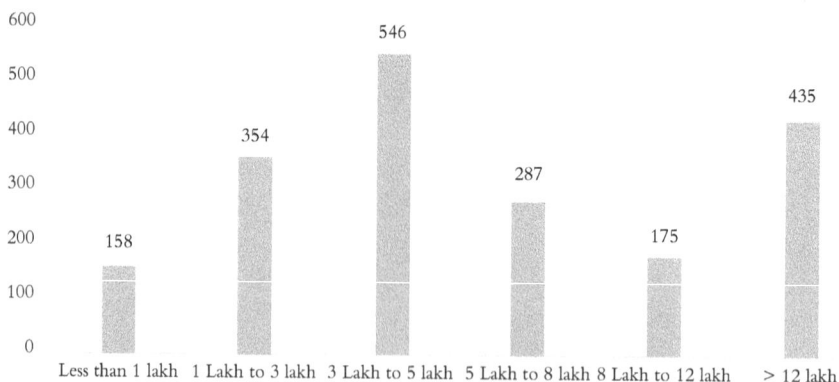

Figure 2.5: Yearly Income of Families (In ₹)

2.6 Type of residence

The study also covered the type of residence of the respondents. The study investigated whether the respondents have their own residence or are living in rented apartments. Figure 2.6 highlights that out of 1955 respondents, (69%) respondents are living in their own houses while (31%) are living in rented apartments. Respondents with rented homes reside close to their educational institutions.

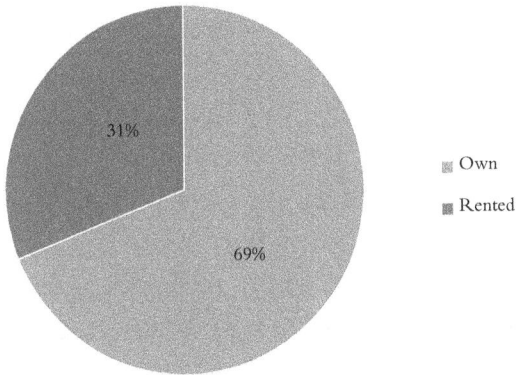

Figure 2.6: Type of residence

Chapter 3
Youth Perceptions

This chapter highlights the perceptions of respondents on mobility related areas such as commuting time, money involved in commuting, consumers satisfaction level with time and money involved, existing problems with public transport system and their safety, perceptions about services which are likely to improve in the near future and their expectations from government policy makers to encourage green transport in their respective cities. It also highlights the policy measures that need to be initiated/strengthened to improve the urban transport system.

Perceptions related to green transport were also recorded to know about current efforts made by respondents. Questions related to mobility of goods and transport system of removal of waste material were also recorded. Respondents also shared their views about priorities that require immediate attention and in a decade for their cities. This chapter also highlights the current challenges faced by citizens in their cities and perceived improvement approaches for the next five years.

3.1 Transport mode used by the respondents

Figure 3.1 explains the frequency of using various transport modes by respondents. Respondents shared their views regarding public transport (bus, metro, shared auto, e-rickshaw) and private transport (scooter, car and auto). The data shows that majority of respondents prefer metro for their daily travel. (31%) of the respondents use bus facilities more than 5 days in a week to commute to their workplace, (29.7%) travel by bus for 2-4 days in a week, (15.4%) travel by bus once in a week, (8.1%) travel by bus once a month and (15.8%) travel by bus every few months. There are close to (40%) respondents who do not use bus facilities on a weekly basis. (35.6%) of the respondents use metro facilities more than 5 days a week to commute to their workplace, (30.1%) travel by metro for 2-4 days in a week, (14.9%) travel by metro once a week, (6.4%) travel by metro once a month and (13.1%) travel in a metro once every few months. There are close to (34%) of the respondents who do not use metro facilities on a weekly basis. The data also revealed that there are (43%) of the respondents who use their scooter once every few months.

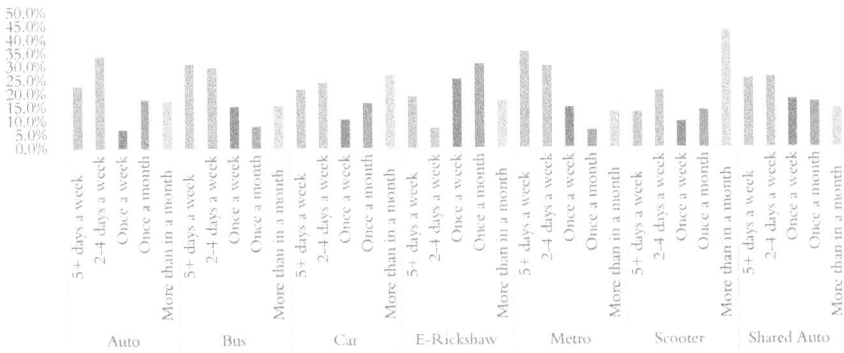

Figure 3.1: Transport mode used by the respondents

3.2 Factors related to mobility

Time to commute

Respondents shared the information regarding time taken to commute from home to destination. Out of the total 1955 respondent surveyed, (34.2%) said that they take less than

30 minutes to travel to their destination. About (35%) said they need between 30 minutes to one hour to commute to their destination while (29%) say it takes them between one to two hours to reach their destination and only (2%) replied that it takes them over two hours. The data revealed that there are a little over two-third of respondents who spend between 30 minutes to over two hours while commuting to their destinations.

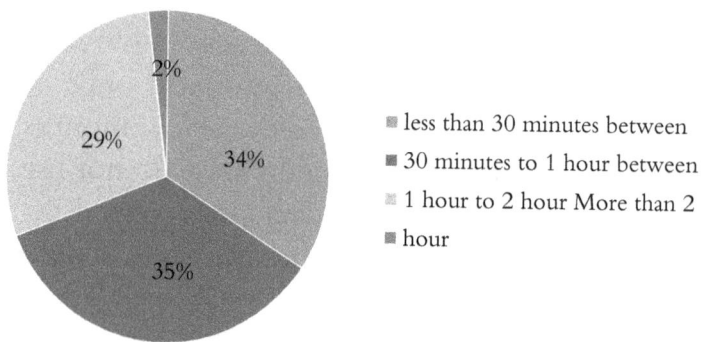

Figure 3.2: Time to commute from home to destination (One side travel)

Monthly expenditure

Figure 3.3 highlights the monthly expenditure incurred by respondents on mobility. The data indicates that (43%) of respondents spend an amount between ₹1001 to ₹3000 on mobility, (26%) of respondents spend less than ₹1000 per month. (15%) respondents said it costs them between ₹3001 to ₹5000 and 15.7% spend above ₹5000 on transport. The data revealed that more than 60% of the respondents spend between ₹1001 to ₹5000. The study highlights that majority of the respondents spend between ₹1001 to ₹3000 per month because many of them belong to low income families (₹3 lakh to ₹5 lakh annually).

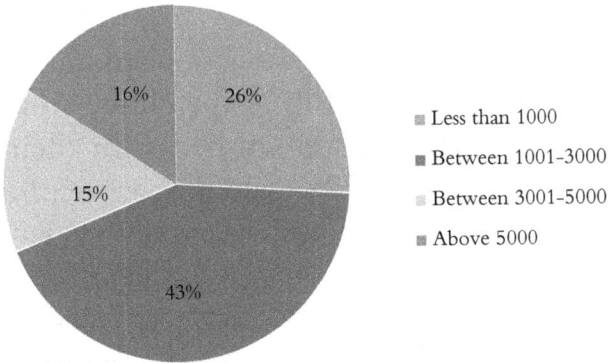

Figure 3.3: Monthly expenditure on mobility (in ₹)

Cost of mobility in next few years

According to Figure 3.4, respondents perceived that there will be an increase in the cost of monthly mobility in the near future, (68%) respondents agree that the cost will increase in near future, (23%) strongly agree, while (7%) disagree and (2%) strongly disagree on the issue. The data highlights that over (90%) of the respondents feel that their expenditure on transport is going to increase in the coming years and this is really an area of concern among them.

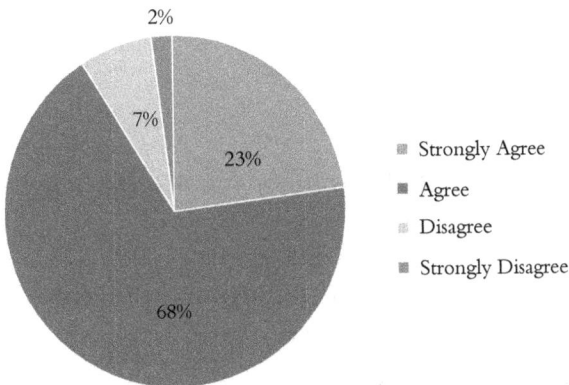

Figure 3.4: Cost of mobility in near future will increase over time

Level of satisfaction

Figure 3.5 shows the level of satisfaction among respondents in relation to their monthly expenditure on mobility. About (38%) respondents are satisfied with their monthly expenditure on mobility. (23%) said they are neither satisfied nor dissatisfied. (13%) respondents are very satisfied and (21%) are dissatisfied with their monthly expenditure on mobility. A very few (6%) said they are very dissatisfied. Here, we can conclude that there is a significant percentage of people who are dissatisfied with their current expenditure on mobility. Subsidized metro tickets for students have not been introduced in the form of passes. The price hike has left students unhappy. They urge for public transport which can save both their time and money.

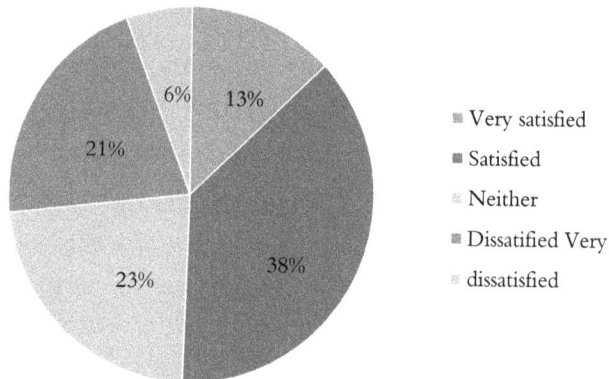

Figure 3.5: Satisfied with the time and money spend

3.3 Problems with public transport

In Figure 3.6, the views regarding problems of public transport system were recorded. Each respondent considered all variables which impacted them the most. Out of the total 1955 respondents, (81.1%) feel that the problem is related to non-reliability especially during non-peak hours. Hence, they do not rely on public transport. About (80.3%) said that the waiting period is too long for their preferred route[1], especially during office hours. (72.4%) said that there are problems related to safety of belongings. The respondents also shared that public buses are often overcrowded and it is not safe for them to travel in buses. A significant percentage of respondents said that last mile connectivity is not available. So, the data in Figure 3.6 indicates that there are multiple problems associated with the public transportation and there is an urgent need to address these problems by the concerned authority at different levels.

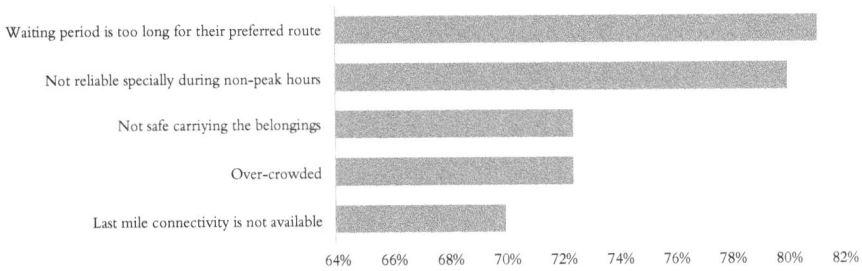

Figure 3.6: Problems with public transport

3.4 Personal safety in public transport

While respondents were asked to rate their personal safety while using public transport, (37%) respondents shared that it is average, (27%) said it is good, very few (12%) feel that the safety measures in public transport are very good. About (15%) said it's poor and (9%) said it's very poor. The study highlights that there is an urgent need for improved safety measures in public transportation because close to (60%) of the respondents felt that the present safety measures are inadequate and they need to be strengthened especially for women and elderly people.

---

1   Here preferred route means the shortest route for commuters between home and destination.

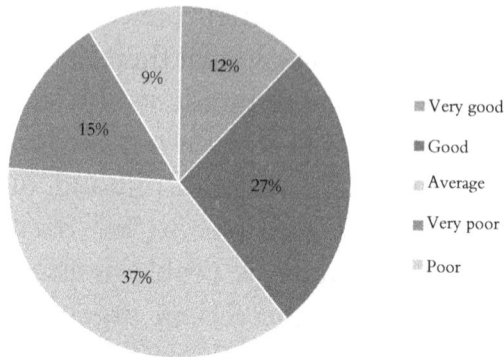

Figure 3.7: Personal safety in public transport

3.5 Services that may improve in the next five years

The data highlights the views of respondents on the services they think will improve in the next five years. (42.1%) of the respondents feel that traffic management will improve to a greater extent. (39.9%) said that parking management will improve to great extent. (35.2%) said that there would be an improvement of bicycle rental and mobility infrastructure to a great extent and (22.2%) said that the car share platform will improve to a great extent.

(33.5%) respondents feel that there will be improvement on bicycle rental and mobility infrastructure. (37.5%) feel the same for charging points for electric cars and (21.1%) feel the same about parking management.

There is a perception among a few respondents that there will be no improvement in any of these areas except traffic management (13.2%). So, it can be concluded from Table 3.1 that the majority of respondents agree that there will be an improvement in the area of car share platform, parking management, bicycle rental and mobility infrastructure, traffic management, management of means of transport, charging points for cars, traceability and logistics application.

Table 3.1: Services that may improve in next five years

N = 1955	To a great extent		To some extent		Somewhat		Very little		Not at all	
	N	N%	N	N%	N	N%	N	N%	N	N%
Bicycle rental and mobility infrastructure	689	35.2%	460	23.5%	654	33.5%	139	7.1%	13	.7%
Car-share platform	434	22.2%	1306	66.8%	160	8.2%	42	2.1%	13	.7%
Charging points for electric cars	297	15.2%	753	38.5%	734	37.5%	171	8.7%	0	0.0%
Management of means of transport	610	31.2%	919	47.0%	350	17.9%	76	3.9%	0	0.0%
Parking management	781	39.9%	641	32.8%	413	21.1%	107	5.5%	13	.7%
Traceability and logistics applications	369	18.9%	1169	59.8%	375	19.2%	42	2.1%	0	0.0%
Traffic management (Detector of free parking places	824	42.1%	575	29.4%	297	15.2%	259	13.2%	0	0.0%

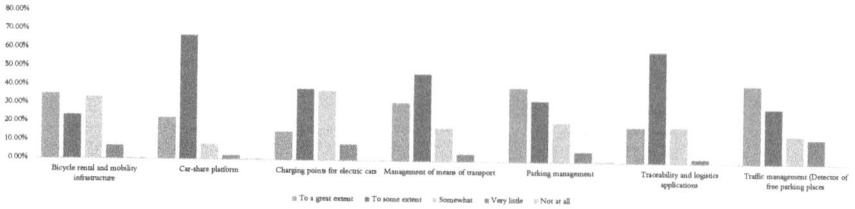

Figure 3.8: Services that may improve in next five years

3.6 Services may improve in the near future

The study highlights that (57.8%) respondents agree with the statement that the public transport system may improve in the near future. About (32.1%) respondents said that in the near future, the availability of shared transport will increase. The lowest priority has been given to private transport because a very small percentage (10.1%) of people use their personal vehicle to travel to their work place.

Table 3.2: Services which may improve in near future

	N = 1955	N%
Public transport	1130	57.8%
Private transport	198	10.1%
Shared transport	627	32.1%

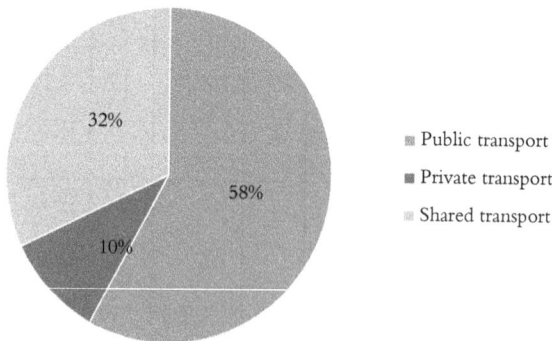

Figure 3.9: Services which will improve in smart cities

3.7 Transport mode that may improve in next five years

When it comes to the question of which mode of public transport is most viable, the study shows that the metro is the best option for majority of the respondents. (54.4%) of respondents feel that the metro is the most convenient and easily available transport source in Delhi. (24.8%) feel that there will be an improvement in road conditions. (13.5%) respondents feel that buses are convenient. The study reveals that metro is the preferred choice over other means of transportation for the majority of respondents. Here, the respondents agreed that metro helps them to avoid traffic and enable them to reach their work places within the stipulated time period as compared to buses and other private transport systems.

Table 3.3: Transport mode that may improve in next five years

N = 1955	N	N%
Buses	264	13.5%
Good roads	484	24.8%
Private Autos	144	7.4%
Trains like Metro	1063	54.4%

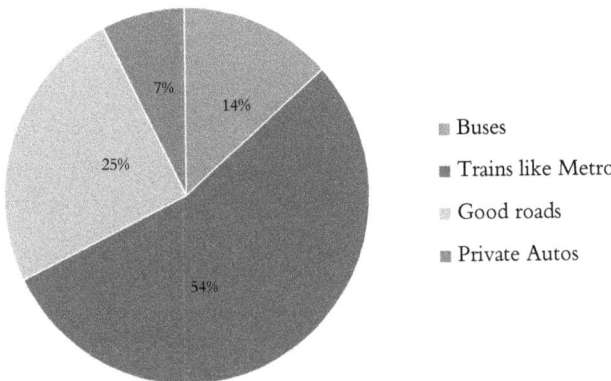

Figure 3.10: Transport mode that may improve in next 5 years

3.8 Willing to pay additional money for better transport

The data mentioned in Table 3.4 shows the willingness of people to pay additional money for better transportation. The data shows that out of total respondents, (40.8%) are willing to pay additional amount up to ₹1000 per month. (37.2%) of respondents can pay additional amount of ₹1001– ₹3000 for daily commuting. (12.3%) of respondents can pay between ₹3001– ₹5000 and (9.7%) can spend more than ₹5000 on public transport. Here, the study reveals that the majority of respondents are willing to spend an additional amount of ₹1001– ₹3000 on public transport provided the transport system is better than the existing one.

Table 3.4: Willing to pay additional money for better transport (Amount in ₹)

N = 1955	N	N%
Less than 1000	798	40.8%
Between 1001–3000	727	37.2%
Between 3001–5000	241	12.3%
Above 5000	189	9.7%

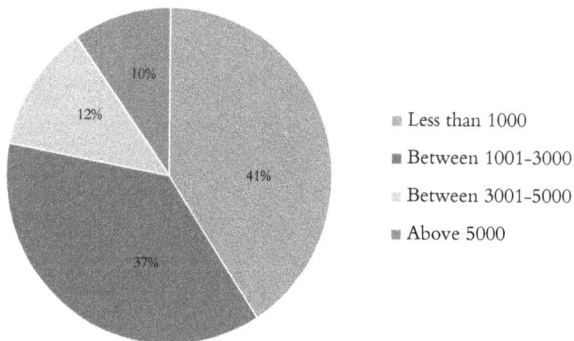

Figure 3.11: Willing to pay additional money for better transport (Amount in ₹)

3.9 Measures for improvement in urban transport system

The data in Figure 3.12 shows that almost all the areas mentioned here are crucial to developing a better transport system for the city. The eight measures which are mentioned in the table are equally important for the respondents to build a sound transport system. Both Delhi-NCR and Lucknow are not adequately equipped with these measures. Measures like restraining the use of polluting vehicles and fuels, promoting car sharing, enhancing transport coordination through real time updates, improving the efficiency of bus transport operations, encouraging green modes of transport and compliance for vehicle emission standards and inspection and maintenance have to be taken into consideration by the government seriously in order to visualize a global smart city.

Table 3.5 shows (87.8%) of respondents have said restraining the use of polluting vehicles and fuels is a crucial measure to promote the green transport. (89.0%) of respondents have also equally emphasized on promoting car sharing/pooling and (85.2%) of respondents feel that enhancing transport coordination through real time updates is important for green transport. The viewers have expressed that the population in Delhi has been increasing since the last two decades and the facilities available are not able to meet the needs of the people. So, in order to provide a good transport system, the government has to take all the initiatives that promote increased usage of the public transport system.

Table 3.5: Measures for improvement in urban transport system

N = 1955	Yes		No	
	N	N%	N	N%
Compliance for vehicle emission standards and inspection and maintenance	1642	84.0%	313	16.0%
Encouraging green modes/ transports	1627	83.2%	328	16.8%

N = 1955	Yes		No	
	N	**N%**	**N**	**N%**
Enhancing transport coordination through real time update	1666	85.2%	289	14.8%
Focusing on public transport particularly bus transport	1593	81.5%	362	18.5%
Improving the efficiency of bus transport operation	1607	82.2%	348	17.8%
Introducing variety of bus transport services	1588	81.2%	367	18.8%
Promoting car sharing/pooling	1739	89.0%	216	11.0%
Restraining the use of polluting vehicles and fuels	1716	87.8%	239	12.2%

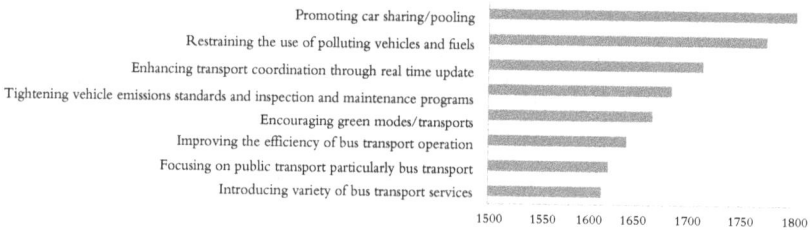

Figure 3.12: Most preferred measures to improve urban transport system

3.10 Perceptions for green transport

The respondents have different views on the use of green transportations and its impact on the environment. The data indicates that most respondents agree to the solutions mentioned for green transport systems. We recorded the opinion of respondents whether they strongly agree, agree, disagree, strongly disagree or are neutral. It is agreed by (52.9%) of respondents that measures like using public transportation, rather than private transport, help to preserve the environment. (28.6%) of respondents strongly agree with this. Similarly, other areas such as green transport are expensive. Many respondents agree that there will be a fall in green transport prices in the near future. A large number of respondents are neutral on these issues. (46.7%) are neutral on the issue of whether green transport is expensive and whether public transport is easy to use (25.5%).

Table 3.6: Perceptions for green transport

N = 1955	Strongly Agree		Agree		Neutral		Disagree		Strongly Disagree	
	N	N%	N	N%	N	N%	N	N%	N	N%
A network of charging facilities is a prerequisite for the use of Green Transport	534	27.30%	696	35.60%	544	27.80%	165	8.40%	16	0.80%
An automobile is a necessity for me	435	22.30%	524	26.80%	532	27.20%	270	13.80%	194	9.90%
Automobiles represent status in society	502	25.70%	648	33.10%	377	19.30%	322	16.50%	106	5.40%
Green transports are expensive	212	10.80%	610	31.20%	913	46.70%	119	6.10%	101	5.20%
I am currently trying my best to reduce car use	658	33.66%	549	28.08%	493	25.22%	204	10.43%	51	2.61%

N = 1955	Strongly Agree		Agree		Neutral		Disagree		Strongly Disagree	
	N	N%	N	N%	N	N%	N	N%	N	N%
More than half of vehicles in India will be replaced by Electric vehicle in 20 years	789	40.40%	510	26.10%	415	21.20%	216	11%	25	1.30%
Public transport is easy to use	587	30%	696	35.60%	499	25.50%	133	6.80%	40	2%
There is no need to reduce car use if I own a Green transport	446	22.80%	671	34.30%	452	23.10%	341	17.40%	45	2.30%
There will be a fall in green transport prices in the near future	261	13.40%	767	39.20%	468	23.90%	343	17.50%	116	5.90%
Using public transportation other than a car helps preserve the environment	559	28.60%	1034	52.90%	94	4.80%	267	13.70%	1	0.10%

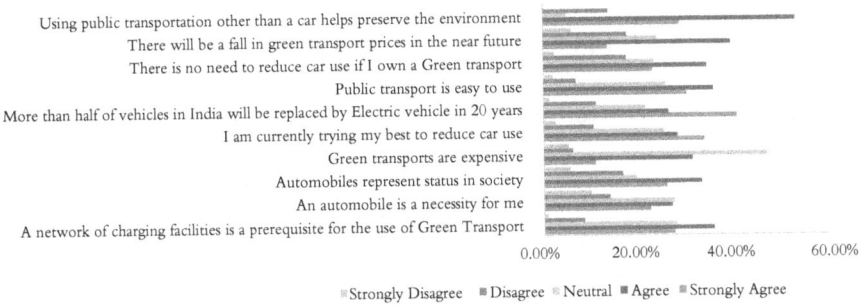

| Using public transportation other than a car helps preserve the environment |
| There will be a fall in green transport prices in the near future |
| There is no need to reduce car use if I own a Green transport |
| Public transport is easy to use |
| More than half of vehicles in India will be replaced by Electric vehicle in 20 years |
| I am currently trying my best to reduce car use |
| Green transports are expensive |
| Automobiles represent status in society |
| An automobile is a necessity for me |
| A network of charging facilities is a prerequisite for the use of Green Transport |

Strongly Disagree ■ Disagree ■ Neutral ■ Agree ■ Strongly Agree

Figure 3.13: Perceptions for green transport

3.11 Suggested measures to promote green transport

Table 3.7 highlights that (89.1%) of respondents have given higher priority to building road networks to support the green transport while (87.2%) respondents prefer infrastructural support by installing charging stations, (87.0%) respondents rely on ensuring a sufficient supply of electricity for each family and (82.6%) of respondents feel that providing subsidy to manufacturers is a good solution. (54.2%) of respondents feel that providing subsidy to consumers is also a better option for green transport, this is a secondary priority compared to other measures.

It can be concluded from the study that Delhi–NCR and Lucknow need to build road networks, infrastructure support and need to supply sufficient electricity for each family in order to support the green transport system which is crucial for future smart cities.

Table 3.7: Suggested measures to promote green transport

N = 1955	Yes		No	
	N	N%	N	N%
By building road network to support the Green Transport	1742	89.10%	213	10.90%
By providing subsidy to consumers	1060	54.20%	895	45.80%

N = 1955	Yes		No	
	N	N%	N	N%
By providing subsidy to manufacturers	1614	82.60%	341	17.40%
Ensuring sufficient supply of electricity for each family	1700	87%	255	13%
Through infrastructural support by installing charging stations	1705	87.20%	250	12.80%

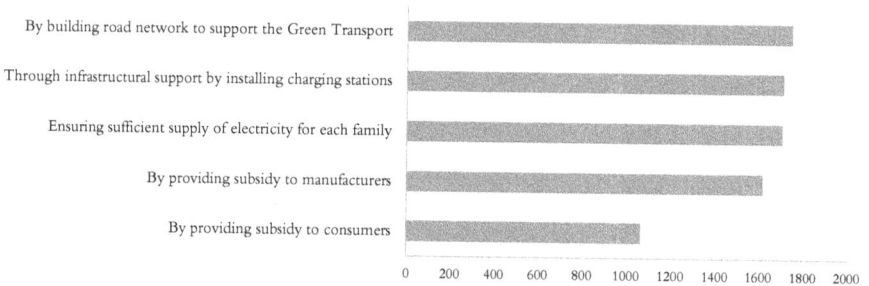

Figure 3.14: Policies for green transport

3.12 Perceptions of efficiency in mobility of goods

Table 3.8 highlights that there is a small percentage of respondents who agree that the mobility of goods in all categories are strongly efficient in the surveyed cities. The data highlights that only (27.42%) of respondents have agreed that mobility of foods and vegetables are very efficient. However, there is a significant percentage of respondents (55.36%) who agree that mobility of manufactured goods[2] is efficient. (49.62%) of respondents feel that mobility is good for food items,[3] (46.5%) agree

---

2   Here, manufactured goods refer to durable goods i.e. Automobile, machinery and semi –manufactured goods i.e. leather, rubber, wood and many more labor-intensive products.

3   Food items includes grocery items, dairy products and other items which are required to prepare food.

on construction material[4] and (46.09%) on packers and movers. Many of the respondents have also expressed that mobility of goods is average. (32.02%) of respondents feel that mobility of packers and movers is average, (30.95%) feel the same for construction material and (29.51%) feel that supply of water is not efficient but average in their function.

Table 3.8: Perceptions of efficiency in mobility of goods

N = 1955	Very efficient		Efficient		Average		Not efficient		Extremely inefficient	
	N	N%	N	N%	N	N%	N	N%	N	N%
Construction material	258	13.20%	910	46.55%	605	30.90%	181	9.26%	1	0.5%
Food items	354	18.11%	970	49.62%	349	17.90%	95	4.86%	187	9.57%
Fruits and vegetables	536	27.42%	894	45.73%	247	12.60%	194	9.92%	84	4.30%
Manufactured goods*	237	12.20%	1075	55.36%	544	28%	84	4.33%	2	0.10%
Packer and movers	247	12.63%	901	46.09%	626	32%	86	4.40%	95	4.86%
Supply of water	290	14.83%	733	37.49%	577	29.50%	230	11.76%	125	6.39%

*N = 1942

---

4   Construction material refers to concrete, cement, steel, sand, wood and many more items which are used in construction work.

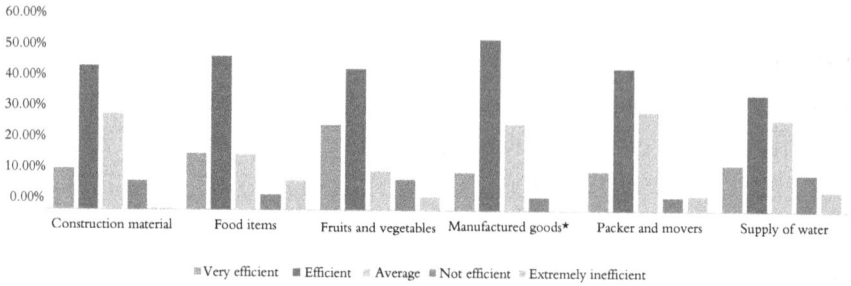

60.00%
50.00%
40.00%
30.00%
20.00%
10.00%
0.00%

Construction material   Food items   Fruits and vegetables   Manufactured goods*   Packer and movers   Supply of water

■Very efficient   ■ Efficient   ▲ Average   ■ Not efficient   » Extremely inefficient

Figure 3.15: Perceptions of efficiency in mobility of goods

3.13 Perceptions about the transport system for removal of waste material

Table 3.9 highlights that majority of the respondents (41.4%) feel that the transport system is efficient for removal of agricultural waste, (34.2%) feel that it is efficient for removal of municipal sources of waste, (33.8%) respondents shared that removal of electronic sources of waste is efficient and (32.4%) view it efficient for removal of industrial sources of waste. The table also shows (23.3%) of respondents have expressed that the transport system is very efficient for the removal of medical/clinical sources of waste and a small percentage of respondents have agreed that the transport system for removal of other waste materials is very efficient. For instance, (15.5%) agreed on industrial sources of waste, (13.5%) on agricultural sources of waste and (12.0%) on construction/demolition sources of waste.

Similarly, in terms of average performance regarding the removal of waste, (39.7%) of respondents shared that the transportation system for removal of electronic sources of waste is average, (33.6%) on construction/demolition sources of waste, (31.1%) on medical/clinical sources of waste followed by other categories. Very few people believe that the transport system for the removal of waste materials in all categories is inefficient. It can be derived from the table that the transport system for removal of waste material is better in the areas of removal of electronic sources of waste and agricultural sources of waste in comparison to other categories.

Table 3.9: Perceptions for transport system for removal of waste material

N = 1955	Very efficient		Efficient		Average		Not efficient		Extremely inefficient	
	N	N%	N	N%	N	N%	N	N%	N	N%
Agricultural sources of waste, N = 1955	263	13.5%	809	41.4%	588	30.1%	215	11.0%	80	4.1%
Con-struction/demolition sources of waste, N = 1955	235	12.0%	561	28.7%	657	33.6%	360	18.4%	142	7.3%
Electronic sources of waste, N = 1955	149	7.6%	660	33.8%	777	39.7%	252	12.9%	117	6.0%
Industrial sources of waste, N = 1955	296	15.1%	633	32.4%	475	24.3%	331	16.9%	220	11.3%
Medical/Clinical sources of waste, N = 1955	466	23.8%	600	30.7%	608	31.1%	211	10.8%	70	3.6%
Municipal sources of waste, N = 1955	310	15.9%	668	34.2%	456	23.3%	453	23.2%	68	3.5%

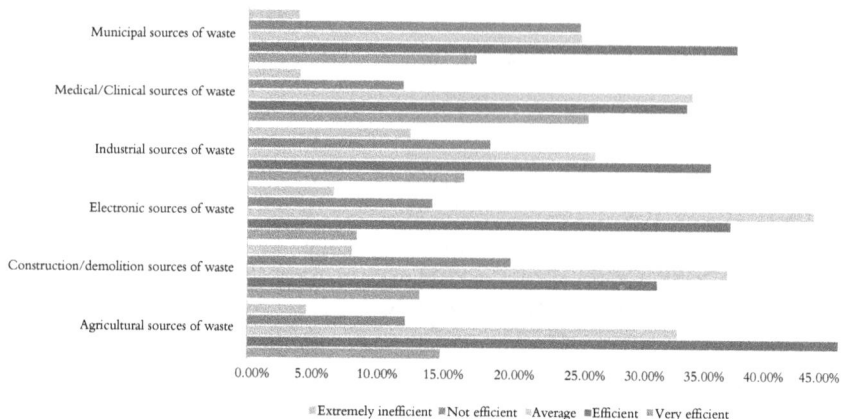

Figure 3.16: Perceptions for transport system for removal of waste material

3.14 Smart Transportation facilities in Smart Cities

Studies show that the public transport's share has reduced from (70%) in 1994 to (40%) in 2007. It is expected to further reduce in the coming years. Lack of quality and safe public transportation, inadequate capacity of public transportation, road safety concerns, overcrowded road network, poor traffic management, parking issues, theft and poor road conditions and lack of modal options (including pedestrian walkways) remain the key issues in most of the cities (Prabhakar, Gupta and Mehrotra 2015). We also asked the respondents about what they are expecting in smart cities.

3.15 Priorities that requires immediate attention and in a decade

The term 'priorities' refers to the various opportunities and facilities likely to be available in a city for a short or long period. Facilities like safety, creative and impactful technology, houses, economic opportunities, education for all, quality health services, better transport system and many more are included in the city vision.

Priorities that require immediate attention

The respondents residing in different cities have expressed their perception about smart cities. It is noteworthy that respondents have expressed their ideas of a smart city as per their background, culture and regions. The ranking has been done on the basis of priorities of respondents regarding various services that are likely to be improved or developed in the short or long term. Priorities that requires immediate attention in a smart city have been ranked as mentioned below:

1. Smart Governance
2. Health facilities for all
3. Houses, Employment and Education for all
4. Smart Infrastructure
5. Clean and Green City

Table 3.10 explains that out of all the total respondents, about (36.38%) have ranked 'Smart Governance' first. Similarly, (36.28%) respondents have given second rank to heath facilities for all, (31.70%) have given third rank to houses, employment and education for all, (29.67%) gave fourth rank to smart infrastructure and (27.94%) gave fifth rank to a clean and green city.

In the immediate requirements, respondents have expressed that smart governance is very crucial for the overall development of a city. They emphasized more on it because in the current situation, the Delhi government has failed to provide safety to women, pollution control measures and better transportation facilities for women and disables. Crime has increased during the last few years within the National Capital Region. The national capital has topped the list in cases of murder, kidnapping and abduction, juveniles in conflict and economic offences. Delhi reported (33%) of total crimes against women (National Crime Record Bureau, 2016). The respondents have also expressed that the current health service system is inadequate to meet the needs of the ever-increasing population. There are inadequate number of public hospitals and health services. The inter-state migration of workers in India has increased substantially to 90 lakhs annually during 2011-16 and the largest recipient of migrant workers was the Delhi region (Economic Survey, 2016-17). Therefore, the respondents viewed that providing houses, employment and education to all is a matter of concern for the state and central government.

Table 3.10: Priorities that requires immediate attention

N = 1955	Count	Rank
Smart Governance	725	1
Health facilities for all	714	2
Houses, Employment and Education for all	624	3
Smart Infrastructure	584	4
Clean and Green City	550	5

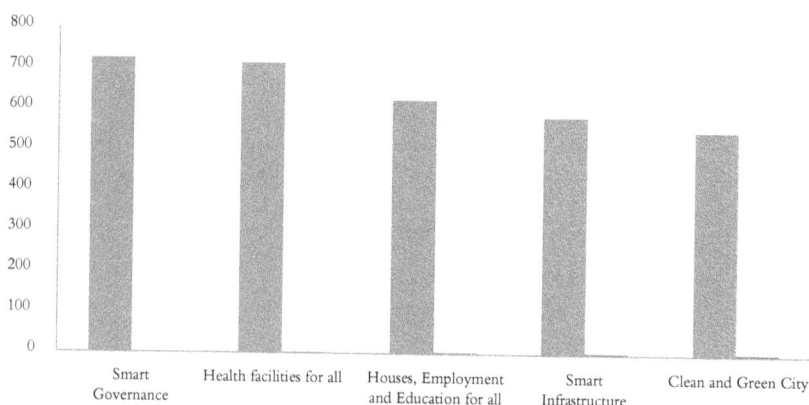

Figure 3.17: Priorities that requires immediate attention

Priorities that require attention in a decade

The respondents have also expressed their perceptions on various priorities which they would like to see in next 10 to 20 years in their city. The priorities are:

1. Availability of House
2. House, employment, education for all
3. Good medical facilities
4. Smart and effective governance and citizen engagement
5. Clean and Green city
6. Develop into world class city consisting of smart and efficient services

1. For priorities that require attention in a decade, (35.82%) of respondents have ranked house, employment, education for all at the first place. They viewed that it is important because in the next 10 to 20 years the population might double due to massive migration. Similarly, on their second priority, (34.6%) of respondents think that increasing population will require more hospitals and quality health services to meet the increased demand. According to respondents, lack of resources, overcrowding and cleanliness would be challenges in the future. Quality healthcare delivery system and health scheme for poor in various localities should be the major concern for the government.

2. (31.04%) of respondents have said that smart and effective governance and citizen engagement plays a significant role in shaping the quality of city life. Citizen engagement through virtual interaction, dialogue and discussions is crucial for urban development which brings attention to local issues and provides suggestions for

solutions. According to the views of respondents, citizen engagement will make sure that the socially, politically, economically and physically disadvantaged citizen get a voice and development projects will be inclusive of these disadvantaged sections.

Table 3.11: Priorities that requires attention in a decade

N = 1955	Count	Rank
House, employment, education for all	705	1
Good medical facilities	682	2
Smart and effective governance and citizen engagement	611	3
Clean and Green city	498	4
Develop into world class city consisting of smart and efficient services	437	5

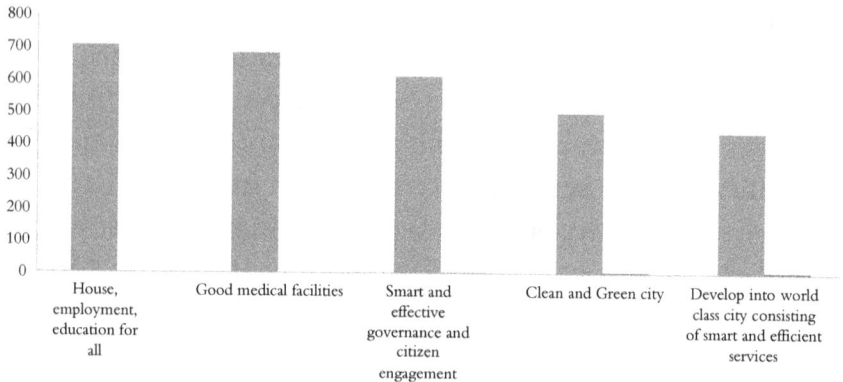

Figure 3.18: Priorities that requires attention in a decade

3.16 Current challenges faced by respondents

Water, sanitation and drainage are critical to urban life. These facilities have direct implication on the health of our economy, society and environment. This section analyses the current state of basic infrastructure in a city and its challenges. Table 3.12 shows the current challenges faced by respondents in a city today. These are significant challenges for development of a smart city. The major challenges as per study in decreasing order are: increasing traffic (92.5%), decline in greenery and cleanliness (81%), increasing housing rate (67.9%), poor governance (68.2%), job opportunities and quality of life (69.7%), increasing crime rates (78.4%), poverty (78.7%) and water related problems (63.1%). Similarly, there are other challenges being faced by the respondents as well. Based on the respondents' views, it is evident that respondents are still facing a lack of basic facilities and those issues need to be addressed at different levels.

Table 3.12: Current challenges faced by youth

N = 1955	Yes		No	
	N	N%	N	N%
Decline in Greenery & Cleanliness	1583	81.0%	372	19.0%
Drop in Cultural values	1302	66.6%	653	33.4%
Energy efficiency (24*7 Electricity)	929	47.5%	1026	52.5%
Fall/drop in tourism	995	50.9%	960	49.1%
Increased crime rates	1533	78.4%	422	21.6%
Increased Traffic	1809	92.5%	146	7.5%
Increasing housing rates	1327	67.9%	628	32.1%
Infrastructure issues (house, roads)	1207	61.7%	748	38.3%
Job opportunities and quality	1363	69.7%	592	30.3%
Lack of Quality of hospitals	1194	61.1%	761	38.9%
Poor governance	1334	68.2%	621	31.8%

N = 1955	Yes		No	
	N	**N%**	**N**	**N%**
Poverty	1539	78.7%	416	21.3%
Rise in pollution	1741	89.1%	214	10.9%
Sewerage/Sanitation issues	1440	73.7%	515	26.3%
Water problems	1233	63.1%	722	36.9%

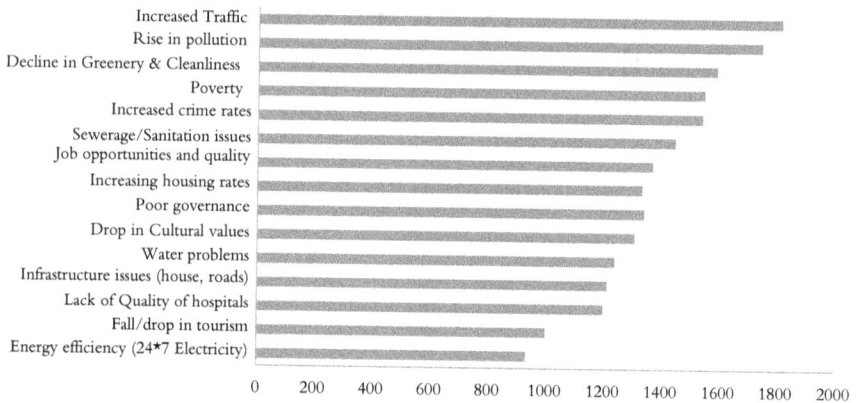

Figure 3.19: Current challenges faced by respondents

3.17 Perceived improvement of challenges in the next five years

Every day, a citizen faces many challenges in their routine life. The challenges are declining greenery & cleanliness, energy efficiency, poverty, quality of hospitals and treatments, governance related issues and many others, but they hope from the civic bodies and government to overcome from these challenges. In this study, the respondents have expressed their views on perceived improvement in challenges in the next five years. Figure 3.20 shows the perceived improvement in challenges in the next five years. As per the study these challenges are going to improve in the coming five years, i.e. greenery and cleanliness (80%), energy efficiency (77%), traffic (41%), increasing housing rate (89%), poor governance (34%), job opportunities and quality (45%), increasing crime rates (45%), sewerage/sanitation issues (34%), increasing pollution level (31.5%), poverty (21%) and water availability (33.8%). Similarly, the figure shows there are other challenges as well.

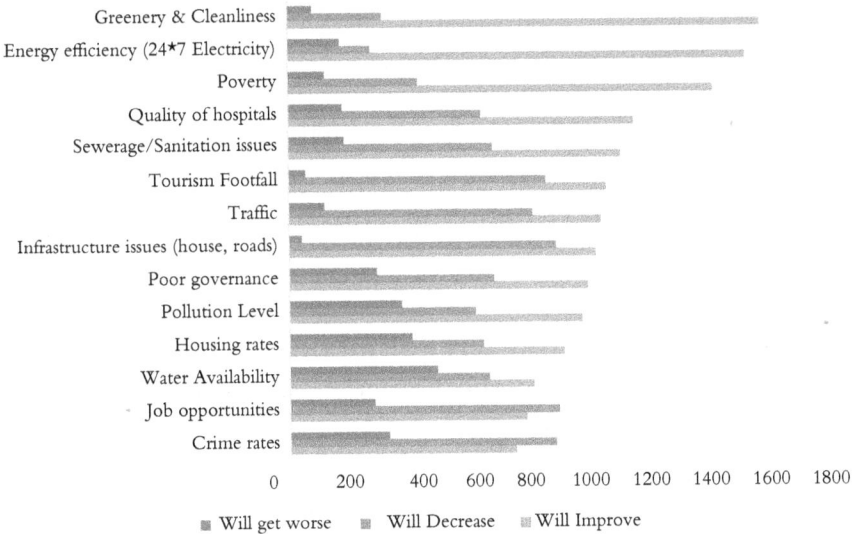

Figure 3.20: Perceived Improvement of challenges in the next five years

To understand more about perceptions, the data was analyzed for Delhi, Gurugram, Noida and Lucknow. The next chapter highlights the regional differences in these perceptions.

Chapter 4
Perceptions based on surveyed cities

This chapter highlights the regional perceptions of youth in mobility-related areas such as commuting time, money involved in commuting, consumers satisfaction level with time and money involved, existing problems with public transport system and their safety, their perceptions for the services which are likely to improve in near future and their expectations from the Government and policymakers to encourage green transport in the cities. It also highlights the policy measures that should be initiated/strengthened to improve the urban transport system. The data was analyzed for Delhi, Gurugram, Noida and Lucknow.

Perceptions related to green transport were also recorded to know the current efforts made by respondents. Questions related to mobility of goods and transport system of removal of waste material were also recorded. Respondents also shared their views about priorities that require immediate attention and in a decade for their cities. This chapter also highlights the current challenges faced by respondents in their cities and perceived improvement approaches for the next five years.

4.1 Transport mode used by respondents

The survey was completed in Delhi, Gurugram, Noida and Lucknow. The total respondents were 1955. The break-up of the responses is as follows – 1117 from Delhi, 403 from Lucknow, 260 from Gurugram and 175 from Noida.

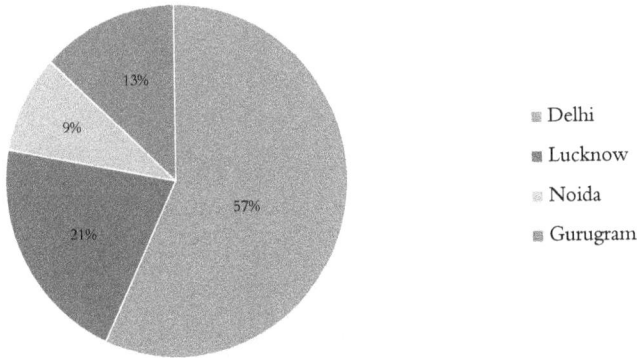

Figure 4.1: Break-up of Respondents by surveyed cities

Table 4.1 shows the frequency for using various transportation modes in Delhi. Here, the transport modes are divided into seven categories such as bus, metro, e-rickshaw, shared auto, scooter, car and auto which are being used by the respondents in their daily life. The data shows that out of 1117 respondents from Delhi, (30.5%) of the respondents take the bus for more than 5 days a week, (29.3%) of the respondents travel by bus for 2-4 days a week, (16.7%) of respondents travel once a week by bus, (8.4%) of the respondents travel once a month by bus, (15%) of respondents travel in bus at least once every few months and data reports that there is not even a single respondent who has not travelled by bus.

The data shows that out of 1117 respondents from Delhi, (33.4%) of respondents take the metro for more than 5 days a week, (31.2%) of the respondents travel for 2-4 days a week, (14.8%) of the respondents travel once a week by metro, (5.9%) of the respondents travel once a month by metro, (13%) of respondents travel by metro at least every few months and data reports that there are (2%) of respondents who have not traveled by metro at all. Data also shows that (42.3%) of the respondents travel by scooter once every few months. This might be because of personal safety and other transport modes available to them.

So, it can be concluded from the data below that in all cases the majority of respondents use metro, bus and auto for their daily mobility. There were very few respondents who said that they do not use metro, bus or auto for daily travel and depend on their personal vehicles.

Table 4.1: Transport mode used by respondents of Delhi

N = 1117	5+ days a week		2-4 days a week		Once a week		Once a month		More than in a month		Not at all	
	N	N%	N	N%	N	N%	N	N%	N	N%	N	N%
Auto	229	20.5%	387	34.6%	90	8.1%	220	19.7%	191	17.1%	0	0%
Bus	341	30.5%	327	29.3%	187	16.7%	94	8.4%	168	15.0%	0	0%
Car	229	20.5%	279	25.0%	138	12.4%	183	16.4%	288	25.8%	0	0%
E-rickshaw	185	16.6%	102	9.1%	270	24.2%	348	31.2%	212	19.0%	0	0%
Metro	373	33.4%	348	31.2%	165	14.8%	66	5.9%	141	12.6%	24	2%
Scooter	131	11.7%	258	23.1%	107	9.6%	148	13.2%	473	42.3%	0	0%
Shared Auto	270	24.2%	280	25.1%	206	18.4%	213	19.1%	148	13.2%	0	0%

Transport mode used by respondents of Gurugram

Table 4.2 shows the frequency of using various public transport modes in Gurugram. The data shows that out of 260 respondents from Gurugram, (30.4%) of the respondents take the bus for more than 5 days a week, (30%) of respondents travel for 2-4 days a week, (15.4%) of respondents travel once a week by bus, (7.3%) of respondents travel once a month by bus, (16.9%) of respondents travel by bus at least every few months and data reports that there is not even a single respondent who has not travelled by bus even once.

The data shows that out of 260 respondents from Gurugram, (35.4%) of respondents take the metro for more than 5 days a week, (29.2%) of respondents travel by metro for 2-4 days a week, (15.4%) of the respondents travel once a week by metro, (5.8%) of respondents travel once a month by metro, (14.2%) of respondents travel by metro at least every few months and data reports that there is not even a single respondent who has not traveled by metro even once. Data also shows that (44.2%) of respondents travel by scooter once every few months. This might be because of personal safety and other transport modes available to them.

Table 4.2: Transport mode used by respondents of Gurugram

N = 260	5+ days a week		2-4 days a week		Once a week		Once a month		More than in a month		Not at all	
	N	N%	N	N%	N	N%	N	N%	N	N%	N	N%
Auto	54	20.8%	91	35.0%	18	6.9%	50	19.2%	47	18.1%	0	0%
Bus	79	30.4%	78	30.0%	40	15.4%	19	7.3%	44	16.9%	0	0%
Car	55	21.2%	65	25.0%	24	9.2%	42	16.2%	74	28.5%	0	0%
E-rickshaw	44	16.9%	21	8.1%	68	26.2%	84	32.3%	43	16.5%	0	0%
Metro	92	35.4%	76	29.2%	40	15.4%	15	5.8%	37	14.2%	0	0%
Scooter	26	10.0%	61	23.5%	26	10.0%	32	12.3%	115	44.2%	0	0%
Shared Auto	69	26.5%	67	25.8%	44	16.9%	43	16.5%	37	14.2%	0	0%

Transport mode used by respondents of Noida

Table 4.3 shows the frequency of using various public transport modes in Noida. The data shows that out of 175 respondents from Noida, (30.9%) of the respondents take the bus for more than 5 days a week, (29.7%) of the respondents travel by bus for 2-4 days a week, (16%) of the respondents travel once a week by bus, (9.1%) of the respondents travel once a month by bus, (14.3%) of the respondents travel by bus at least every few months and data reports that there is not even a single respondent who has not travelled by bus even once.

The data also shows that out of 175 respondents from Noida, (36%) of the respondents take the metro for more than 5 days a week, (30.9%) of the respondents travel by metro for 2-4 days a week, (14.3%) of the respondents travel once a week by metro, (6.9%) of the respondents travel once a month by metro, (12%) of the respondents travel by metro at least every few months.

So, it can be concluded from table 4.3 that the majority of respondent use metro, bus and auto for their everyday mobility.

Table 4.3: Transport mode used by respondents of Noida

N=175	5+ days a week		2-4 days a week		Once a week		Once a month		More than in a month		Not at all	
	N	N%	N	N%	N	N%	N	N%	N	N%	N	N%
Auto	40	22.9%	66	37.7%	14	8.0%	27	15.4%	28	16.0%	0	0%
Bus	54	30.9%	52	29.7%	28	16.0%	16	9.1%	25	14.3%	0	0%
Car	39	22.3%	41	23.4%	24	13.7%	28	16.0%	43	24.6%	0	0%
E-rickshaw	32	18.3%	21	12.0%	41	23.4%	49	28.0%	32	18.3%	0	0%
Metro	63	36.0%	54	30.9%	25	14.3%	12	6.9%	21	12.0%	0	0%
Scooter	30	17.1%	36	20.6%	16	9.1%	28	16.0%	65	37.1%	0	0%
Shared Auto	44	25.1%	44	25.1%	34	19.4%	28	16.0%	25	14.3%	0	0%

Transport mode used by respondents of Lucknow

Table 4.4 shows the transport modes used by respondents of Lucknow. The data shows that in Lucknow majority of respondents use shared autos, cars, e-rickshaws and scooters to travel to their destinations. The use of bus transport in Lucknow is not that significant. Data shows that only (6.5%) of the respondents travel by bus weekly. The metro was not operational at the time of the survey so the responses for Lucknow are not applicable.

It can be analyzed that e-rickshaw and shared auto play a major role in mobilizing people in Lucknow in comparison to other public transport.

Table 4.4: Transport mode used by respondents of Lucknow

N=403	5+ days a week		2-4 days a week		Once a week		Once a month		More than in a month		Not at all	
	N	N%	N	N%	N	N%	N	N%	N	N%	N	N%
Bus	28	7%	27	7%	26	6%	159	39%	95	24%	68	17%
Metro★	0	0%	0	0%	0	0%	0	0%	0	0%	377	100%
Shared Auto	110	27%	55	14%	26	6%	118	29%	67	17%	27	7%
E-rick-shaw	124	31%	68	17%	13	3%	66	16%	118	29%	14	3%
Scoot-er★★	136	35%	54	14%	52	13%	13	3%	28	7%	107	27%
Car★★	93	24%	81	21%	41	11%	40	10%	41	11%	94	24%
Auto★★	68	17%	83	21%	41	11%	13	3%	93	24%	92	24%

★ N = 377, ★★ N = 390

4.2 Monthly expenditure of respondents on mobility

Table 4.5 shows the monthly expenditure of respondents on mobility. The data indicates that in Delhi, (17.4%) of respondents spend an amount between ₹3001 – ₹5000 per month for commuting. (48.4%) spend between ₹1001– ₹3000 per month and (22.6%) spend less than ₹1000 per month. A significant percentage of respondents (11.5%) spend above

₹5000 a month. The argument here is that many respondents included in the study are unemployed and belong to middle class/lower middle-class families. They do not want to spend more on traveling and often choose to stay at places close to their travel destination.

Similarly, in Gurugram, (17%) of respondents have said that they spend between ₹3001 - ₹5000 for commuting. (48%) said they spend between ₹1001 - ₹3000. Around (23%) spend less than ₹1000 every month.

In Noida, (16%) of respondents have stated that they spend an amount between ₹3001 - ₹5000, (46.3%) spend between ₹1001 - ₹3000 and (22.9%) spend less than ₹1000 per month.

In Lucknow, the scenario is a bit different from Delhi and Gurugram. In Lucknow, (29.8%) respondents have stated that they spend above ₹5000 per month. Approximately (36.9%) spend less than ₹1000 and only (6.7%) between ₹3001 - ₹5000.

Table 4.5: Monthly expenditure of respondents on mobility

Amount in ₹	Delhi N = 1117		Gurugram N = 260		Noida N = 175		Lucknow N = 403	
	N	N%	N	N%	N	N%	N	N%
Less than 1000	253	22.6%	60	23%	40	22.9%	149	36.9%
Between 1001-3000	541	48.4%	125	48%	81	46.3%	107	26.6%
Between 3001-5000	194	17.4%	44	17%	28	16.0%	27	6.7%
Above 5000	129	11.5%	31	12%	26	14.9%	120	29.8%

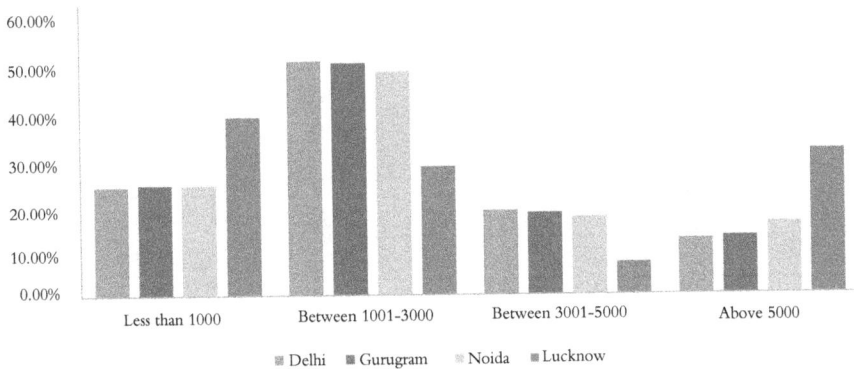

Figure 4.2: Monthly expenditure of respondents on mobility (amount in ₹)

Increase in monthly expenditure for commuting

When questions were asked about the increase in monthly expenditure for commuting in coming times, in Delhi, (68.6%) respondents agree that the cost will increase in future, (23.9%) strongly agree with this while (6%) and (1.5%) respectively said that they disagree and strongly disagree with it. In Gurugram, (69.2%) respondents agree with the increase in traveling cost, (24.2%) strongly agree and (5.4%) of respondents disagree with this perception. In Noida, (66.9%) respondents agree with the increase in expenditure. (25.7%) strongly agree, (4.6%) respondents disagree and (2.9%) strongly disagree with the statement. Similarly, in Lucknow (66.3%) respondents agree with the increase in commuting expenditures, (16.9%) strongly agree (13.4%) disagree and (3.5%) strongly disagree.

Respondents have replied that the key reasons behind the increase in commuting expenditure will be a hike in price rate of petrol and energy in all cities. Insufficient public transport and shortage of availability are some other reasons for increase in mobility cost in future.

Table 4.6: Cost of mobility in near future will increase over time in surveyed cities

	Delhi		Gurugram		Noida		Lucknow	
	N = 1117		N = 260		N = 175		N = 403	
	N	N%	N	N%	N	N%	N	N%
Strongly Agree	267	23.9%	63	24.2%	45	25.7%	68	16.9%
Agree	766	68.6%	180	69.2%	117	66.9%	267	66.3%
Disagree	67	6.0%	14	5.4%	8	4.6%	54	13.4%
Strongly Disagree	17	1.5%	3	1.2%	5	2.9%	14	3.5%

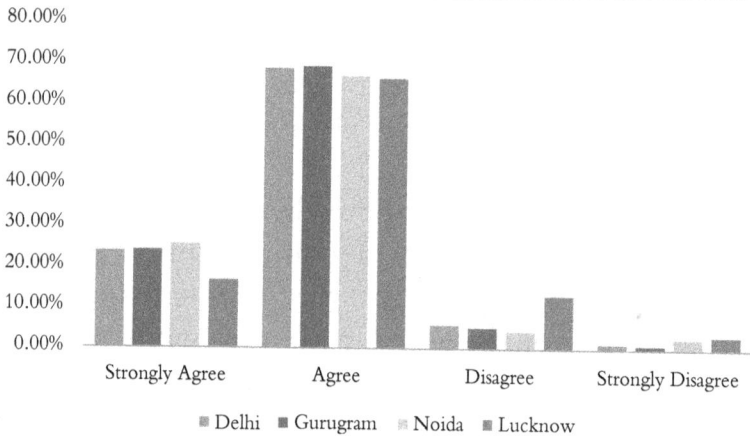

Figure 4.3: Cost of mobility in near future will increase over time in surveyed cities

Level of satisfaction in relation to monthly expenditure

Table 4.7 explains the level of satisfaction of respondents in relation to their monthly expenditure on mobility. In Delhi, about (13.7%) respondents have replied that they are very satisfied with their monthly expenditure on mobility. (40.3%) are satisfied with the expenditure, (24.4%) are neither satisfied nor very satisfied. (20.1%) respondents are dissatisfied and (1.5%) are very dissatisfied with their monthly expenditure on travel.

In Gurugram, about (26.2%) of respondents have stated that they are neither satisfied nor very satisfied with their monthly expenditure on travel, (12.7%) are very satisfied and (38.5%) are satisfied with their monthly expenditure on mobility.

In Noida, (13.7%) of respondents have replied that they are very satisfied with their monthly travel expenses, (26.9%) are neither satisfied nor very satisfied, (38.3%) of respondents have said they are satisfied and (18.3%) are dissatisfied.

In Lucknow, (23.1%) of respondents have stated that they are very dissatisfied with their monthly travel expense, (26.1%) are dissatisfied, (31.3%) are satisfied and (16.1%) are neither satisfied nor very satisfied with their monthly expenditure on mobility.

Hence, we can conclude that there is a significant percentage of people who are dissatisfied with their current expenditure on mobility. They urge for the kind of public transport which can save both their time and money.

Table 4.7: Satisfied with the time and money spend

	Delhi		Gurugram		Noida		Lucknow	
	N = 1117		N = 260		N = 175		N = 403	
	N	N%	N	N%	N	N%	N	N%
Very satisfied	153	13.7%	33	12.7%	24	13.7%	14	3.5%
Satisfied	450	40.3%	100	38.5%	67	38.3%	126	31.3%
Neither	272	24.4%	68	26.2%	47	26.9%	65	16.1%
Dissatisfied	225	20.1%	56	21.5%	32	18.3%	105	26.1%
Very dissatisfied	17	1.5%	3	1.2%	5	2.9%	93	23.1%

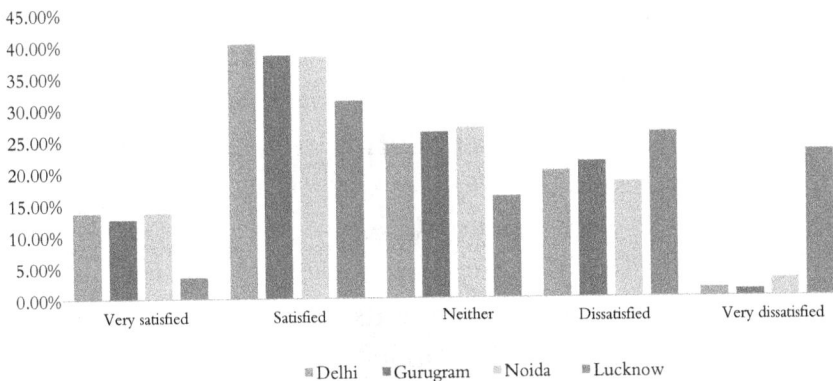

Figure 4.4: Satisfied with the time and money spend

4.3 Problems with public transport

Table 4.8 explains the problems of public transportation in the four cities under study. Out of the total respondents in Delhi, (95.6%) said that the problem is related to waiting period, which is too long for preferred route. (93.2%) think that non-reliability of public transport especially during non–peak hours is the major problem and (85.6%) think that public transport is not safe for belongings and an equal percentage of people also think that non–availability for last mile connectivity is also a major problem. About (78.3%) of respondents have viewed that the vehicles are generally overcrowded.

In Gurugram (100%) of respondents have said that the major problem is related to waiting period which is too long for preferred route. (97.3%) people believe non-reliability, especially during non–peak hours, is a big problem. (88.5%) think that last mile connectivity is not available, (87.3%) feel that their belongings are not safe in public transport and (74.6%) said that the vehicles are generally overcrowded.

In Noida, (100%) of respondents view waiting period as a major issue which is too long for preferred route. (97.7%) shared that non-reliable especially during non–peak hours is major issue, (87.3%) mentioned safety of belongings as a major issue and (83.4%) shared that vehicles are generally overcrowded.

In Lucknow, (49.6%) of respondents feel that the major problem is related to overcrowded public transport. (29.8%) think non-reliable especially during non–peak hours is the major problem and (19.9%) feel that safety of belongings in public transport is the major issue.

Please note that the respondents have voted for multiple issues. Hence, the data represents that there are multiple problems associated with public transportation in all the cities and the concerned government must address these challenges at different levels.

Table 4.8: Problems with Public Transport

	Delhi		Gurugram		Noida		Lucknow	
	N = 1117		N = 260		N = 175		N = 403	
	N	N%	N	N%	N	N%	N	N%
Last mile connectivity is not available	956	85.60%	230	88.50%	133	76%	53	13.20%
Over – crowded	875	78.30%	194	74.60%	146	83.40%	200	49.60%
Not safe for carrying the belongings	956	85.60%	227	87.30%	153	87.40%	80	19.90%
Not reliable specially during non-peak hours	1041	93.20%	253	97.30%	171	97.70%	120	29.80%
Waiting period is too long for correct route	1068	95.60%	260	100%	175	100%	66	16.40%

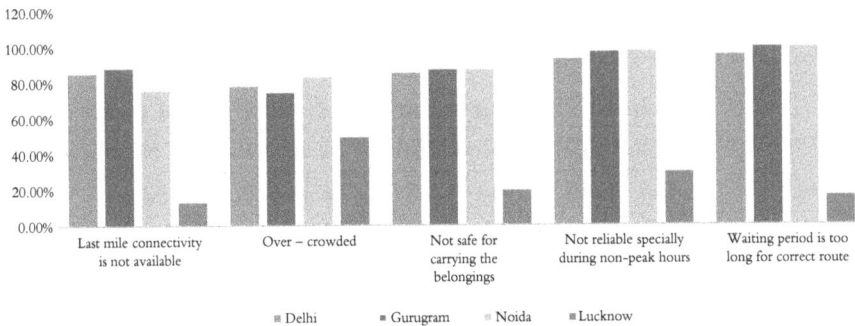

Figure 4.5: Problems with Public Transport

4.4 Personal safety in public transport

When respondents were asked about their personal safety when travelling by public transport and given five options to rate their views, in Delhi, (12.7%) respondents have replied that the safety measures in public transport are very good, (29.2%) replied it is good about (39.5%) said its average and (14.1%) said it is poor. The study reveals that there are still some requirements of safety measures in public transportation because a significant percentage of respondents have viewed the present safety measures as inadequate and feel that they need to be developed more, especially for women and elderly people.

In Gurugram, (13.1%) respondents have stated that safety measures in public transport are very good, (30.8%) replied good, (38.5%) think it's average and (14.6%) said it's poor. In Noida, (12.6%) respondents have viewed safety measures in public transport as very good, (26.3%) replied it's average, (41.7%) good and (13.7%) said it's poor.

In Lucknow, (6.4%) respondents have viewed that the safety measures in public transport is very good, (17.3%) replied its average, (29.7%) good and (19.6%) said it is poor. (26.8%) of respondents from Lucknow shared that personal safety is very poor.

Table 4.9: Personal safety in public transport

	Delhi		Gurugram		Noida		Lucknow	
	N = 1117		N = 260		N = 175		N = 403	
	N	N%	N	N%	N	N%	N	N%
Very good	142	12.7%	34	13.1%	22	12.6%	26	6.4%
Good	326	29.2%	80	30.8%	46	26.3%	70	17.3%
Average	441	39.5%	100	38.5%	73	41.7%	120	29.7%
Poor	157	14.1%	38	14.6%	24	13.7%	79	19.6%
Very Poor	51	4.6%	8	3.1%	10	5.7%	108	26.8%

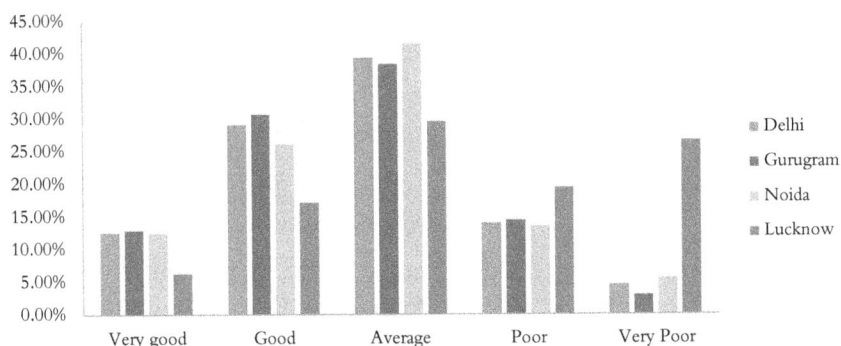

Figure 4.6: Personal safety in public transport

4.5 Services that will improve in next five years

Table 4.10 highlights the views of the respondents related to the services that will improve in the next five years. There are several issues categorically mentioned here and each issue has its own significance to develop a world class smart city. Respondents were given four choices to rate the services that will improve in the next five years. The respondents had to rate them on whether the services will improve to a great extent, somewhat, very little and not at all.

In Delhi, (43.2%) of respondents said that traffic management will improve to great extent, (38.9%) said that parking management will improve to great extent. (39.8%) said the same about bicycle rental and mobility infrastructure and (33.2%) feel the same about management of means of transport. Similarly, (68.7%) respondents feel that car share platform will improve somewhat, (60.3%) think the same for traceability and logistics applications, (44.5%) on management of means of transport and (40.1%) on charging points for electric cars. The study also reveals that for (20.9%) of respondents, there will be little improvement on bicycle rental and mobility infrastructure and (26.9%) feel the same for traffic management (Detector for free parking places).

Moreover, in Gurugram (45.8%) of respondents have shared that traffic management will improve to greater extent, (40.0%) said that parking management will improve to a great extent. (38.8%) respondents feel the same for improvement of bicycle rental and mobility infrastructure and (33.1%) feel the same for management of means of transport. Similarly, (72.7%) respondents have viewed that there will be some improvement on car share platform, (63.5%) feel it for traceability and logistics applications, (46.5%) for management of means of transport and (43.1%) for charging points for electric cars. The study also reveals that (21.5%) of respondents viewed that there will be little improvement on bicycle rental and mobility infrastructure and (25%) feel the same for traffic management (Detector for free parking places).

Similarly, in Noida (42.3%) of respondents viewed that bicycle rental and mobility infrastructure will improve to a great extent, (41.7%) viewed the same for traffic management, (38.9%) on parking management and (33.1%) on management of means of transport. Similarly, (69.7%) of respondents have viewed that there will be some improvement on car share platform, (58.9%) on traceability and logistic applications, (41.7%) on management of means of transport and (33.4%) on parking management. (20%) feel that that there will be a little improvement on bicycle rental and mobility infrastructure, (27.4%) feel the same about traffic management (Detector for free parking places). The study also shows that there is a small percentage of respondents who have replied that there will be no improvement in these areas except traffic management.

Furthermore, in Lucknow, (45.9%) said the parking management will improve to a greater extent, (37.2%) said that traffic management will improve to a great extent and (23.6%) respondents feel the same for management of means of transport. Similarly, (56.6%) of respondents have viewed that car share platform will improve somewhat, (56.6%) feel the same for traceability and logistics applications, (56.6%) for management of means of transport and (40.0%) for traffic management (Detector for free parking places).

So, it can be concluded from the table that the majority of respondents have agreed that there will be an improvement in the area of car share platform, traceability and logistic applications, traffic management, bicycle rental and mobility infrastructure.

Table 4.10: Services that may improve in next five years★

	Delhi N = 1117		Gurugram N = 260		Noida N = 175		Lucknow N = 403	
	To a Great Extent	Some-what	To a Great Extent	Some-what	To a Great Extent	Some-what	To a Great Extent	Some-what
Bicycle rental and mobility infrastructure	39.8%	20.9%	38.8%	20.3%	33.7%	21.5%	42.3%	20.0%
Car-share platform	23.2%	68.7%	20.0%	23.8%	56.6%	72.7%	22.9%	69.7%
Charging points for electric cars	14.9%	40.1%	12.7%	17.1%	33.5%	43.1%	16.6%	33.1%
Management of means of transport	33.2%	44.5%	33.1%	23.6%	56.6%	46.5%	33.1%	41.7%
Parking management	38.9%	32.1%	40.8%	45.9%	37.2%	29.6%	38.9%	31.4%
Traceability and logistics applications	18.6%	60.3%	16.9%	20.1%	56.6%	63.5%	20.6%	58.9%
Traffic management (Detector of free parking places)	43.2%	26.9%	45.8%	37.2%	40.0%	25.0%	41.7%	27.4%

★*Response for very little and not at all has been removed from the data considering the importance of other variables*

4.6 Services may improve in near future

Table 4.11 shows the different kinds of transport systems and views of respondents regarding improved transport in the future in a smart city. The study highlights that (39.3%) of respondents in Delhi agree that the shared transport would serve the real purpose of a large population because majority of them depend on shared transport in their everyday life. The government of Delhi has also come up with new plans and strategies to make public transport more convenient for the people of Delhi. About (49.5%) of respondents have responded that public transport services may be improved in near future, as significant percentage of people also use public transport for their daily traveling within the city. The lowest percentage is on private transport. In case of Gurugram, out of all the respondents covered, (53.5%) have said that public transport will be better in a future smart city, (36.5%) have supported shared transport. In Noida, (50.3%) have said that public transport will be better in a future smart city, (38.3%) have supported shared transport.

Similarly, in Lucknow, about (86.8%) of viewers have expressed that public transport will be better in a smart city and (6.5%) have supported shared transport.

Table 4.11: Services which may improve in near future

	Delhi		Gurugram		Noida		Lucknow	
	N = 1117		N= 260		N=175		N = 403	
	N	N%	N	N%	N	N%	N	N%
Public transport	553	49.5%	139	53.5%	88	50.3%	350	86.8%
Private transport	125	11.2%	26	10.0%	20	11.4%	27	6.7%
Shared transport	439	39.3%	95	36.5%	67	38.3%	26	6.5%

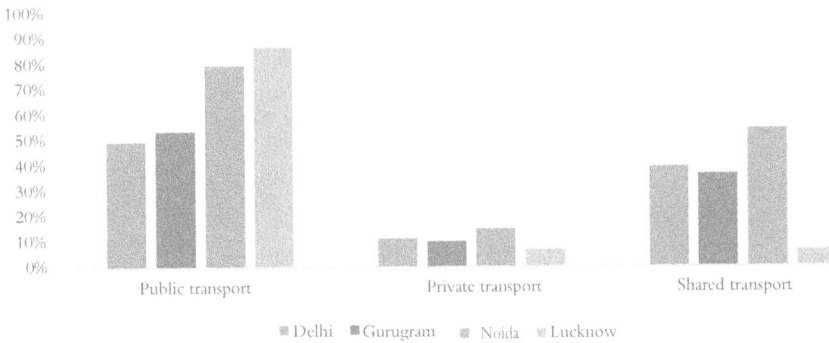

Figure 4.7: Services which may improve in near future

4.7 Transport mode that might improve in the next five years

Table 4.12 highlights transport modes that might improve in next five years. More than (50%) of respondents in all surveyed cities shared that rapid transit system like Metro is going to be the best mode of transport. Here, respondents have viewed that the metro helps them to avoid traffic and they are able to reach their work places in stipulated time as compared to buses and other private transports.

Table 4.12: Transport mode that may improve in next five years

	Delhi		Gurugram		Noida		Lucknow	
	N = 1117		N= 260		N=175		N = 403	
	N	N%	N	N%	N	N%	N	N%
Buses	192	17.20%	45	17.30%	27	15.43%	0	0.00%
Trains like Metro	589	52.70%	143	55.00%	90	51.43%	241	59.80%
Good roads	227	20.30%	53	20.40%	42	24.00%	162	40.20%
Private Autos	109	9.80%	19	7.30%	16	9.14%	0	0.00%

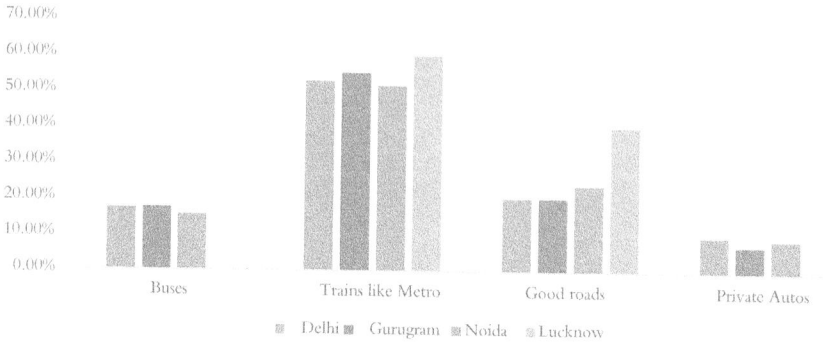

Figure 4. 8: Transport mode that may improve in next five years

4.8 Willing to pay additional money for better transport

Table 4.13 explains the willingness of respondents to pay additional money for better transport. The data shows that there is no significant difference between perceptions of respondents from Delhi, Gurugram and Noida. However, the respondents from Lucknow are not willing to spend the amount between ₹3001 – ₹5000. There are (45.9%) respondents from Lucknow who are willing to spend an additional amount of ₹1001– ₹3000 and (17.3%) of the respondents from the same city can spend an amount of more than ₹5000 in a month.

Table 4.13: Willing to pay additional money for better transport (Amount in ₹)

Amount in ₹	Delhi N = 1117		Gurugram N = 260		Noida N = 175		Lucknow N = 403	
	N	N%	N	N%	N	N%	N	N%
Less than 1000	465	41.63%	110	42.31%	75	42.86%	148	36.72%
Between 1001–3000	394	35.27%	89	34.23%	59	33.71%	185	45.91%
Between 3001–5000	173	15.49%	39	15.00%	29	16.57%	0	0.00%
Above 5000	85	7.61%	22	8.46%	12	6.86%	70	17.37%

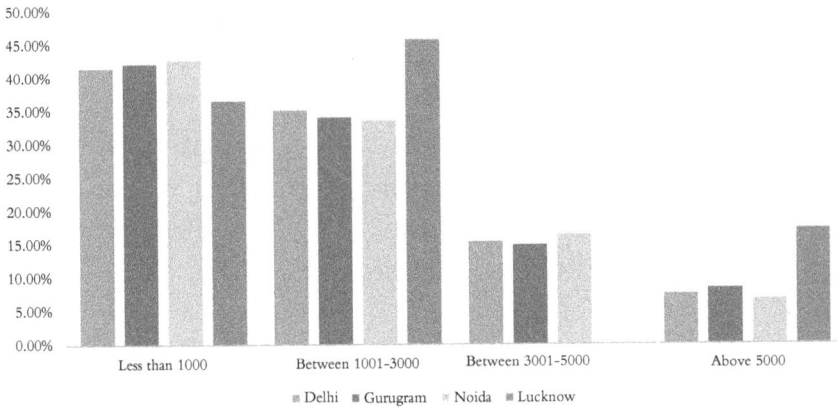

Figure 4.9: Willing to pay additional money for better transport (Amount in ₹)

4.9 Perceptions for green transport

Table 4.14 below explains the regional views on policies for green transport. In Delhi, (100%) of respondents shared that policies for green transport can be supported by building better road networks, (98.6%) of respondents emphasized on providing subsidy to manufacturers, (97.9%) on ensuring sufficient supply of electricity for each family and (97%) viewers have agreed on infrastructural support by installing charging stations.

In Gurugram, (100%) respondents have stated that policies for green transport can be supported by building better road networks and providing infrastructural support by installing charging stations, (98.6%) think that it can be done by providing subsidies to manufacturers and (99.6%) think it can be done by ensuring sufficient supply of electricity for each family.

In Noida, (100%) respondents have expressed that policies for green transport can be supported by building better road networks, an equal percentage of people support providing subsidies to manufacturers, infrastructural support by installing charging stations and (99.4%) think it can be done by ensuring sufficient supply of electricity for each family.

Similarly, in Lucknow, (47.1%) of respondents shared that policies for green transport can be supported by building better road networks, (46.4%) emphasize on infrastructural support by installing charging stations, (42.9%) support on ensuring sufficient supply of electricity for each family and (29.8%) emphasized on providing subsidies to consumers.

Table 4.14: Perceptions for green transport

	Delhi N = 1117		Gurugram N= 260		Noida N=175		Lucknow N = 403	
	N	N%	N	N%	N	N%	N	N%
By providing subsidy to consumers	672	60.2%	158	60.8%	110	29.8%	120	29.8%
By providing subsidy to manufacturers	1101	98.6%	259	99.6%	175	19.6%	79	19.6%
Through infrastructural support by installing charging stations	1083	97.0%	260	100.0%	175	46.4%	187	46.4%
By building road network to support the Green Transport	1117	100.0%	260	100.0%	175	47.1%	190	47.1%
Ensuring sufficient supply of electricity for each family	1094	97.9%	259	99.6%	174	42.9%	173	42.9%

4.10 Measures for improvement in urban transport systems

Table 4.15 shows that almost all the areas mentioned here are crucial to develop a smart city particularly in the area of transportation. The eight measures which are mentioned in the table are equally important for the respondents to build a sound transport system and many of the studied cities are not adequately equipped with these measures. These measures are:

- Focusing on public transit transport, particularly metro
- Introducing variety of bus transport services on different routes
- Improving the efficiency of bus transport operation
- Enhancing transport coordination through real time update
- Promoting car sharing/pooling
- Restraining the use of polluting vehicles and fuels
- Compliance for vehicle emission standards and inspection and maintenance
- Encouraging green modes/transports

Measures like restraining the use of polluting vehicles and fuels, promoting car sharing, enhancing transport coordination through real time updates, improving the efficiency of bus transport operations, encouraging green modes/transports and compliance for vehicle emission standards and inspection and maintenance have to be taken in to consideration by the government seriously in order to visualize a global smart city.

The table shows, in Delhi, (98.4%) of respondents have said that restraining the use of polluting vehicles and fuels are crucial measures to promote green transport, (97.6%)

emphasized on compliance for vehicle emission standards and inspection and maintenance, (97.5%) agreed on introducing variety of bus transport services and (97.2%) emphasized on enhancing transport coordination through real time updates and encouraging green modes/transports respectively.

In Gurugram, (100%) of respondents said that introducing a variety of bus transport services, improving the efficiency of bus transport operations, compliance for vehicle emission standards, inspection and maintenance and encouraging green modes/transports are important. (99.6%) of respondents expressed that enhancing transport coordination through real time updates is necessary, (99.6%) voted for promoting car sharing/pooling and (99.6%) for restraining the use of polluting vehicles and fuels.

In Noida, as well, (100%) respondents emphasized on improving the efficiency of bus transport operation and encouraging green modes/transports respectively. About (99.4%) respondents mentioned enhancing transport coordination through real time updates, promoting car sharing/ pooling, restraining the use of polluting vehicles and fuels and compliance for vehicle emission standards and inspection and maintenance is crucial for better urban transport systems.

Similarly, in Lucknow, (56.1%) of respondents expressed that promoting car sharing/pooling is crucial for urban transportation, (45.7%) emphasized on restraining the use of polluting vehicles and fuels, (36.5%) of respondents emphasized on enhancing transport coordination through real time updates and (29.3%) on compliance for vehicle emission standards and inspection and maintenance.

The respondents also expressed that there has been an increase in population in urban areas in last two decades and the available facilities are not able to meets the needs of the people. So, in order to provide a good transport system, the government has to take all the initiatives that promote public transport systems.

Table 4.15: Measures for improvement in urban transport system

	Delhi		Gurugram		Noida		Lucknow	
	N = 1117		N= 260		N=175		N = 403	
	N	N%	N	N%	N	N%	N	N%
Compliance for vehicle emission standards and inspection and maintenance	1090	97.60%	260	100%	174	99.40%	118	29.30%
Encouraging green modes/ transports	1086	97.20%	260	100%	175	100%	106	26.30%
Enhancing transport coordination through real time update	1086	97.20%	259	99.60%	174	99.40%	147	36.50%
Focusing on public transport particularly bus transport	1067	95.50%	250	96.20%	171	97.70%	105	26.10%
Improving the efficiency of bus transport operation	1078	96.50%	260	100%	175	100%	94	23.30%
Introducing variety of bus transport services	1089	97.50%	260	100%	174	99.40%	65	16.10%
Promoting car sharing/pooling	1080	96.70%	259	99.60%	174	99.40%	226	56.10%
Restraining the use of polluting vehicles and fuels	1099	98.40%	259	99.60%	174	99.40%	184	45.70%

4.11 Perceptions for green transport

Respondents were asked 10 questions on green transport and rate them as strongly agree, agree, neutral, disagree and strongly disagree. The survey was done in all four cities taken into consideration. The total respondents were 1955. The break-up of the responses is as follows – 1117 from Delhi, 260 from Gurugram, 175 from Noida and 403 from Lucknow.

Delhi

Table 4.16 shows the perceptions of the respondents for green transport in Delhi. The respondents have different views on use of transportation and its impact on the environment. The data shows that the mentioned areas for green transport are almost agreed by the respondents. For instance, in Delhi, the contention that using public transportation, rather than a car, helps preserve the environment is agreed by (51.7%) of respondents and strongly agreed by (32%). Similarly, (38.2%) said that public transport is easy to use, (33.2%) viewed there will be a fall in green transport prices in the near future, where more respondents have agreed but not strongly agreed. There are also a larger number of respondents who are neutral on these issues, like (49.8%) of respondents are neutral on the subject that green transports are expensive and (28.9%) said an automobile is a necessity for them. The data also explains that there is a small percentage of respondents who disagree or strongly disagree with all the mentioned areas. For instance, (21%) of respondents disagree with the perception that, there is no need to reduce car use if they own green transport and (20.1%) disagree that there will be a fall in green transport prices in the near future. Out of the total respondents, about (12.1%) strongly disagree with the perception that an automobile is a necessity for them.

Table 4.16: Perceptions for green transport

N = 1117	Delhi									
	Strongly Agree		Agree		Neutral		Disagree		Strongly Disagree	
	N	N%	N	N%	N	N%	N	N%	N	N%
A network of charging facilities is a prerequisite for the use of Green Transport	328	29.4%	398	35.6%	286	25.6%	95	8.5%	10	.9%
An automobile is a necessity for me.	192	17.2%	282	25.2%	323	28.9%	182	16.3%	138	12.4%
Automobiles represent status in society.	312	27.9%	337	30.2%	174	15.6%	221	19.8%	73	6.5%
Green transports are expensive.	115	10.3%	304	27.2%	556	49.8%	73	6.5%	69	6.2%
I am currently trying my best to reduce car use	425	38.0%	356	31.9%	229	20.5%	107	9.6%	0	0.0%
More than half of vehicles in India will be replaced by Electric vehicle in 20 years	461	41.3%	246	22.0%	248	22.2%	145	13.0%	17	1.5%
Public transport is easy to use.	343	30.7%	427	38.2%	263	23.5%	84	7.5%	0	0.0%
There is no need to reduce car use if I own a Green transport.	247	22.1%	358	32.1%	247	22.1%	235	21.0%	30	2.7%

N = 1117	Delhi									
	Strongly Agree		Agree		Neutral		Disagree		Strongly Disagree	
	N	N%	N	N%	N	N%	N	N%	N	N%
There will be a fall in green transport prices in the near future.	180	16.1%	371	33.2%	268	24.0%	225	20.1%	73	6.5%
Using public transportation other than a car helps preserve the environment	357	32.0%	577	51.7%	50	4.5%	132	11.8%	1	.1%

Gurugram

In Gurugram, (42.3%) respondents strongly agree with the statement that more than half the vehicles in India will be replaced by electric vehicles in 20 years. (39.6%) strongly agree with the point that they are currently trying their best to reduce car use, (31.2%) strongly agree with the point that public transport is easy to use and (30.8%) strongly agree that a network of charging facilities is a prerequisite for the use of green transport. Table 4.31 also shows about (54.6%) of respondents agreed that using public transportation rather than a car helps preserve the environment, (36.9%) agree that public transport is easy to use, (34.6%) agree that a network of charging facilities is a prerequisite for the use of green transport and (33.5%) agree that there will be a fall in green transport prices in the near future. People also have neutral views on certain topics, (53.5%) of respondents are neutral on the issue that green transport is expensive and (29.2%) are neutral on the point that an automobile is a necessity for them. There are other areas as well where the respondents have taken a neutral position. The data also shows that about (21.9%) of respondents disagree with the statement that there is no need to reduce car use if they own a green transport and (20.4%) disagree that there will be a fall in green transport prices in the near future. Similarly, about (13.1%) of respondents strongly disagree that an automobile is a necessity for them and (7.7%) strongly disagree that there will be a fall in green transport prices in the near future.

Table 4.17: Perceptions for green transport

N = 260	Gurugram									
	Strongly Agree		Agree		Neutral		Disagree		Strongly Disagree	
	N	N%	N	N%	N	N%	N	N%	N	N%
A network of charging facilities is a prerequisite for the use of Green Transport	80	30.8%	90	34.6%	63	24.2%	23	8.8%	4	1.5%
An automobile is a necessity for me.	41	15.8%	62	23.8%	76	29.2%	47	18.1%	34	13.1%
Automobiles represent status in society.	71	27.3%	75	28.8%	45	17.3%	52	20.0%	17	6.5%
Green transports are expensive.	25	9.6%	58	22.3%	139	53.5%	19	7.3%	19	7.3%

N = 260	Gurugram									
	Strongly Agree		Agree		Neutral		Disagree		Strongly Disagree	
	N	N%	N	N%	N	N%	N	N%	N	N%
I am currently trying my best to reduce car use	103	39.6%	76	29.2%	54	20.8%	27	10.4%	0	0.0%
More than half of vehicles in India will be replaced by Electric vehicle in 20 years	110	42.3%	51	19.6%	58	22.3%	38	14.6%	3	1.2%
Public transport is easy to use.	81	31.2%	96	36.9%	61	23.5%	22	8.5%	0	0.0%
There is no need to reduce car use if I own a Green transport.	59	22.7%	75	28.8%	61	23.5%	57	21.9%	8	3.1%
There will be a fall in green transport prices in the near future.	37	14.2%	87	33.5%	63	24.2%	53	20.4%	20	7.7%
Using public transportation other than a car helps preserve the environment	77	29.6%	142	54.6%	7	2.7%	34	13.1%	0	0.0%

Noida

Table 4.18 explains the perception of respondents in Noida on automobile and green transport. In Noida, (41.1%) of respondents strongly agree that they are currently trying their best to reduce car use, (40.6%) strongly agree that half of the vehicles in India will be replaced by electric vehicles in 20 years, (32.6%) strongly agree that using public transportation rather than a car helps preserve the environment and (30.3%) strongly agree with the point that public transport is easy to use. The table also shows that about (50.9%) of respondents have agreed that using public transportation rather than a car helps preserve the environment, (37.7%) agree that public transport is easy to use, (34.3%) agree that there is no need to reduce car use if they own green transport and (33.4%) agree on there will be a fall in green transport prices in the near future. People also have neutral views with (48.6%) of respondents neutral on the fact that green transport is expensive, (29.1%) are neutral on the issue of whether an automobile is a necessity for them, (28.0%) are neutral on whether a network of charging facilities is a prerequisite for the use of green transport and (24.6%) are neutral on the point that there will be a fall in green transport prices in the near future. There are other areas as well where the respondents have taken a neutral stand or have agreed or strongly agreed which is displayed in the table. The data also shows that about (21.7%) of respondents have disagreed that there will be a fall in green transport prices in the near future, (20.0%) disagree that there is no need to reduce car use if they own a green transport and automobiles represent status in society. About (12%) respondents strongly disagree with the perception that an automobile is a necessity for them.

Table 4.18: Perceptions for green transport

N = 175	Noida									
	Strongly Agree		Agree		Neutral		Disagree		Strongly Disagree	
	N	N%	N	N%	N	N%	N	N%	N	N%
Using public transportation other than a car helps preserve the environment	57	32.6%	89	50.9%	10	5.7%	19	10.9%	0	0.0%
I am currently trying my best to reduce car use	72	41.1%	49	28.0%	38	21.7%	16	9.1%	0	0.0%
A network of charging facilities is a prerequisite for the use of Green Transport	47	26.9%	58	33.1%	49	28.0%	19	10.9%	2	1.1%
An automobile is a necessity for me.	30	17.1%	44	25.1%	51	29.1%	28	16.0%	22	12.6%
Automobiles represent status in society.	53	30.3%	45	25.7%	26	14.9%	35	20.0%	16	9.1%
Green transports are expensive.	18	10.3%	46	26.3%	85	48.6%	13	7.4%	13	7.4%
More than half of vehicles in India will be replaced by Electric vehicle in 20 years	71	40.6%	38	21.7%	42	24.0%	19	10.9%	5	2.9%

N = 175	Noida									
	Strongly Agree		Agree		Neutral		Disagree		Strongly Disagree	
	N	N%	N	N%	N	N%	N	N%	N	N%
Public transport is easy to use.	53	30.3%	66	37.7%	43	24.6%	13	7.4%	0	0.0%
There is no need to reduce car use if I own a Green transport.	35	20.0%	60	34.3%	38	21.7%	35	20.0%	7	4.0%
There will be a fall in green transport prices in the near future.	30	17.1%	55	31.4%	43	24.6%	38	21.7%	9	5.1%

Lucknow

Table 4.19 explains the perceptions of respondents on automobile and green transport in Lucknow. Here, (42.7%) of respondents strongly agree that an automobile is a necessity for them, (36.5%) strongly agree that more than half of the vehicles in India will be replaced by electric vehicles in 20 years, (23.7%) strongly agree on the point that public transport is easy to use and (26.1%) strongly agree that there is no need to reduce car use if they own a green transport. The table also shows that about (63%) of respondents agree on the point that there will be a fall in green transport prices in the near future, (56.1%) agree that using public transportation rather than a car helps preserve the environment, (50.1%) agree that green transport is expensive, (47.4%) agree on automobiles represent status in society and (43.4%) agree that more than half of vehicles in India will be replaced by electric vehicle in 20 years. When it comes to the point of neutral views,

(44.1%) of respondents are neutral on the fact that they are currently trying their best to reduce car use, (36.2%) are neutral on the fact that a network of charging facilities is a prerequisite for the use of green transport, (32.8%) are neutral on the contention that automobiles represent status in society and (32.8%) are neutral on the point that public transport is easy to use. There are other areas as well where the respondents have taken a neutral position, agreed and strongly agreed which is mentioned in the table. The data also shows that about (20.3%) of respondents have disagreed on the point that using public transportation rather than a car helps preserve the environment and (13.8%) disagree that they are currently trying their best to reduce car use. There is a very few percentage of respondents who strongly disagree with the given perceptions.

Table 4.19: Perceptions for green transport

	Lucknow, N = 403									
	Strongly Agree		Agree		Neutral		Disagree		Strongly Disagree	
	N	N%	N	N%	N	N%	N	N%	N	N%
A network of charging facilities is a prerequisite for the use of Green Transport	79	19.6%	150	37.2%	146	36.2%	28	6.9%	0	0.0%
An automobile is a necessity for me.	172	42.7%	136	33.7%	82	20.3%	13	3.2%	0	0.0%
Automobiles represent status in society.	66	16.4%	191	47.4%	132	32.8%	14	3.5%	0	0.0%

	Lucknow, N = 403									
	Strongly Agree		Agree		Neutral		Disagree		Strongly Disagree	
	N	N%	N	N%	N	N%	N	N%	N	N%
Green transports are expensive.	54	13.4%	202	50.1%	133	33.0%	14	3.5%	0	0.0%
I am currently trying my best to reduce car use	54	13.8%	68	17.4%	172	44.1%	54	13.8%	42	10.8%
More than half of vehicles in India will be replaced by Electric vehicle in 20 years	147	36.5%	175	43.4%	67	16.6%	14	3.5%	0	0.0%
Public transport is easy to use.	110	27.3%	107	26.6%	132	32.8%	14	3.5%	40	9.9%
There is no need to reduce car use if I own a Green transport.	105	26.1%	178	44.2%	106	26.3%	14	3.5%	0	0.0%
There will be a fall in green transport prices in the near future.	14	3.5%	254	63.0%	94	23.3%	27	6.7%	14	3.5%

	Lucknow, N = 403									
	Strongly Agree		Agree		Neutral		Disagree		Strongly Disagree	
	N	N%	N	N%	N	N%	N	N%	N	N%
Using public transportation other than a car helps preserve the environment	68	16.9%	226	56.1%	27	6.7%	82	20.3%	0	0.0%

4.12 Perceptions of efficiency in mobility of goods

Respondents were asked to give their views on green transport, 10 questions were asked and respondents were asked to rate them as strongly agree, agree, neutral, disagree and strongly disagree. A survey was done in all the four cities taken into consideration. The total respondents were 1955. The break-up of the responses is as follows – 1117 from Delhi, 260 from Gurugram, 175 from Noida and 403 from Lucknow.

Perceptions of efficiency in mobility of goods – Delhi

Respondents were asked to give their opinion about mobility of goods in various categories and rate them as very efficient, efficient, average, not efficient and extremely inefficient. As per table 4.20, only (27.8%) of respondents agree that the mobility of fruits and vegetables in the city is very efficient, (17.0%) of respondents think the same about food items, (14%) about construction material and (10.7%) about manufactured goods. A significant percentage of people agree that the mobility of goods in Delhi in various categories is efficient. (55.5%) of respondents have viewed the mobility of manufactured goods as efficient, (51.3%) think the same about food items, (48.9%) about packers and movers and

(40.1%) about fruits and vegetables. Many respondents have also expressed that the mobility of goods is average. For instance, (35.6%) respondents have viewed that mobility of construction material is average, (32.2%) think the same about water supply and (29.4%) about packers and movers. About (11.9%) of respondents have expressed that water supply is not efficient, (11.5%) think the same about construction material and (11.4%) about fruits and vegetables. The data also shows that about (11.6%) of respondents have replied that mobility of food items and water supply is extremely inefficient.

Table 4.20: Perceptions of efficiency in mobility of goods - Delhi

	Delhi									
N=1117	**Very efficient**		**Efficient**		**Average**		**Not efficient**		**Extremely inefficient**	
	N	**N%**	**N**	**N%**	**N**	**N%**	**N**	**N%**	**N**	**N%**
Construction material, N = 1116	156	14.0%	434	38.9%	398	35.6%	128	11.5%	1	.1%
Food items, N = 987	190	17.0%	573	51.3%	157	14.1%	67	6.0%	130	11.6%
Fruits and Vegetables, N = 1058	310	27.8%	448	40.1%	173	15.5%	127	11.4%	59	5.3%
Manufac-tured goods, N = 1115	120	10.7%	620	55.5%	317	28.4%	58	5.2%	2	.2%
Packer and Movers, N = 1050	114	10.2%	546	48.9%	328	29.4%	62	5.6%	67	6.0%
Supply of water, N = 1028	109	9.8%	426	38.1%	360	32.2%	133	11.9%	89	8.0%

Perception of efficiency related to mobility of goods – Gurugram

Table 4.21 indicates the perceptions about efficiency related to mobility of goods in Gurugram. The data explains that only (28.5%) of respondents have agreed that mobility of fruits and vegetables is very efficient, (15.4%) feel the same for food items, (13.5%) about construction material and (11.2%) about manufactured goods. But there is a significant percentage of respondents who agree that the mobility of goods in Gurugram is efficient. For instance, the data reveals that (56.9%) of respondents have viewed the mobility of manufactured goods as efficient in Gurugram, (55.4%) feel the same about food items, (48.5%) about packers and movers and (40.8%) about fruits and vegetables. Out of the total respondents, (34.2%) of respondents have viewed mobility of construction material as average, (30.8%) feel the same about supply of water and (29.6%) about packers and movers. When it comes to the question of these movements being not efficient and extremely inefficient, about (12.7%) said that mobility of construction material is not efficient, followed by (11.9%) who think that supply of water is not efficient and (12.3%) think the same about mobility of fruits and vegetables. The data also shows that about (13.1%) of respondents said that mobility of food items is extremely inefficient and (8.5%) said supply of water is extremely inefficient in Gurugram.

Table 4.21: Perceptions of efficiency in mobility of goods - Gurugram

N = 260	Gurugram									
	Very efficient		Efficient		Average		Not efficient		Extremely inefficient	
	N	N%	N	N%	N	N%	N	N%	N	N%
Con-struction material	35	13.5%	103	39.6%	89	34.2%	33	12.7%	0	0.0%

N = 260	Gurugram									
	Very efficient		Efficient		Average		Not efficient		Extremely inefficient	
	N	N%	N	N%	N	N%	N	N%	N	N%
Food items	40	15.4%	144	55.4%	25	9.6%	17	6.5%	34	13.1%
Fruits and Vegetables	74	28.5%	106	40.8%	33	12.7%	32	12.3%	15	5.8%
Manu-factured goods	29	11.2%	148	56.9%	70	26.9%	13	5.0%	0	0.0%
Packer and Movers	27	10.4%	126	48.5%	77	29.6%	16	6.2%	14	5.4%
Supply of water	26	10.0%	101	38.8%	80	30.8%	31	11.9%	22	8.5%

Perceptions of efficiency in mobility of goods – Noida

Table 4.22 explains the perceptions about efficiency related to mobility of goods in Noida. The data displays that only (32%) of respondents have agreed that mobility of fruits and vegetables is very efficient, (23.4%) think the same for food items and (15%) for construction material. The table also shows that there are large number of respondents who agree that the mobility of goods in Noida is efficient. (54.9%) of respondents have viewed that mobility of manufactured goods is efficient, (46.9%) feel it efficient for packers and movers, (45.7%) for food items and (37.1%) for construction materials. Out of the total respondents, (36%) of respondents have replied mobility of construction material is average, (31.4%) feel it average for water supply, (28%) for packers and movers and (27.4%) for manufactured goods. When it comes to the question of not efficient and extremely inefficient, about (14.3%) of respondents have said that the supply of water is not efficient, (12.6%) feel it not efficient for fruits and vegetables. The figure also shows that about (13.1%) of respondents have viewed the mobility for food items and mobility of packers and movers (8.0%) as extremely inefficient.

Table 4.22: Perceptions of efficiency in mobility of goods - Noida

N = 175	Noida									
	Very efficient		Efficient		Average		Not efficient		Extremely inefficient	
	N	N%	N	N%	N	N%	N	N%	N	N%
Con-struction material	27	15.4%	65	37.1%	63	36.0%	20	11.4%	0	0.0%
Food items	41	23.4%	80	45.7%	20	11.4%	11	6.3%	23	13.1%
Fruits and Vegetables	56	32.0%	60	34.3%	27	15.4%	22	12.6%	10	5.7%
Manu-factured goods	18	10.3%	96	54.9%	48	27.4%	13	7.4%	0	0.0%
Packer and Movers	22	12.6%	82	46.9%	49	28.0%	8	4.6%	14	8.0%
Supply of water	21	12.0%	60	34.3%	55	31.4%	25	14.3%	14	8.0%

Perceptions of efficiency in mobility of goods – Lucknow

Table 4.23 explains the perceptions about efficiency related to mobility of goods in Lucknow. The data shows that only 33.3% of respondents have agreed that the mobility for supply of water is very efficient in Lucknow, 23.8% think the same about fruit and vegetables and 20.8% about packers and movers. The data also indicates that a large number of respondents have agreed that mobility of goods in Lucknow is efficient, 76.4% respondents have expressed that mobility of construction and material manufactured goods is efficient, followed by 69.5% who think that mobility of fruits and vegetables is efficient, 54.1% think the same for manufactured goods and 42.9% for food items. Out of the total respondents, 13.6% of respondents have viewed that mobility of construction material is average, 20.3% think it average for water supply and 42.7% for packers and movers. When it comes to the question of not efficient and extremely inefficient, about 3.2% feel that mobility of fruits and vegetables is not efficient, 10.2% think the same for water supply.

Table 4.23: Perceptions of efficiency in mobility of goods – Lucknow

N = 403	Lucknow									
	Very efficient		Efficient		Average		Not efficient		Extreme-ly ineffi-cient	
	N	N%	N	N%	N	N%	N	N%	N	N%
Con-struction material	40	9.9%	308	76.4%	55	13.6%	0	0.0%	0	0.0%
Food items	83	20.6%	173	42.9%	147	36.5%	0	0.0%	0	0.0%
Fruits and Vegetables	96	23.8%	280	69.5%	14	3.5%	13	3.2%	0	0.0%
Manu-factured goods*	70	17.9%	211	54.1%	109	27.9%	0	0.0%	0	0.0%
Packer and Movers	84	20.8%	147	36.5%	172	42.7%	0	0.0%	0	0.0%
Supply of water	134	33.3%	146	36.2%	82	20.3%	41	10.2%	0	0.0%

*N = 390

4.13 Perceptions about the transport system for removal of waste material

Management of timely removal of waste material is critical to improving the efficiency of the cities. It becomes necessary to understand the perceptions of youth regarding the transport system for removal of various type of waste material such as municipal waste, medical/clinical waste, agricultural waste, industrial waste, construction/demolition waste and electronic waste so that the civic bodies can be sensitized and efficient transport mechanism can be developed.

Perceptions for transport system for removal of waste material – Delhi

In Delhi, (46%) respondents have viewed that the transport system is efficient for removal of agricultural waste, (35.2%) feel that it is efficient for municipal waste, (33.4%) think the same for electronic waste, (31.3%) feel the same for industrial waste, (24.5%) think it is efficient to remove medical/clinical waste and (13.9%) feel it efficient for agricultural waste.

Table 4.24 shows that not many respondents have agreed that the transport system to remove other wastage materials is very efficient. When it comes to the question of average performance, (43.2%) of respondents feel it is average for electronic waste, (32.2%), (25.8%) and (25.5%) feel the same for construction/demolition waste, industrial waste and medical/clinical waste respectively. When it comes to the question of not efficient or extremely inefficient transport system for removal of waste in different categories, there is percentage number of respondents who think that transport systems are not efficient. For instance, (27.8%) of respondents have replied that the mobility for municipal waste is inefficient, (19.1%) feel the same for construction/demolition waste and

(16.6%) for industrial waste. About (13.9%) of respondents have viewed the mobility of industrial waste as extremely inefficient. It can be derived from the table that transport system for removal of waste material in Delhi is better in the areas of electronic waste and agricultural waste as compared to other categories. The state authority should address the concerned challenges and pay attention to those transport systems that are inefficient in the removal of waste materials within the city.

Table 4.24: Perceptions for transport system for removal of waste material - Delhi

N = 1117	Delhi									
	Very efficient		Efficient		Average		Not efficient		Extremely inefficient	
	N	N%	N	N%	N	N%	N	N%	N	N%
Agricultural sources of waste	155	13.9%	514	46.0%	248	22.2%	144	12.9%	56	5.0%
Construc-tion/demo-lition sources of waste	144	12.9%	308	27.6%	360	32.2%	213	19.1%	92	8.2%
Electronic sources of waste	59	5.3%	373	33.4%	483	43.2%	130	11.6%	72	6.4%
Industrial sources of waste	139	12.4%	350	31.3%	288	25.8%	185	16.6%	155	13.9%
Medical/ Clinical sources of waste	274	24.5%	368	32.9%	285	25.5%	140	12.5%	50	4.5%
Municipal sources of waste	175	15.7%	393	35.2%	190	17.0%	310	27.8%	49	4.4%

Perceptions for transport system for removal of waste material – Gurugram

Table 4.25 explains the perception about transport systems for removal of waste material in Gurugram. In Gurugram, (46.9%) of respondents have replied that the transport system is efficient for the removal of agricultural waste, (33.1%) feel it is efficient for municipal waste, (31.5%) think it is efficient for electronic waste and industrial waste respectively. The table also shows that (26.2%) of respondents think that the transport system is very efficient for the removal of medical/clinical waste, (14.6%) feel it very efficient for municipal waste and (12.7%) feel the same for construction/demolition waste.

When it come to the question of average performance, the figure shows that (45%) of respondents have viewed the performance as average for electronic waste, (32.3%) feel the same for construction/demolition waste, (25.4%) about medical/clinical waste and (24.6%) about industrial waste. When it comes to the question of not efficient or extremely inefficient transport systems, (30.0%) of respondents have said that the mobility for municipal waste is inefficient, (21.5%) think it is inefficient for construction/demolition waste and (18.1%) feel the same about industrial waste. About (13.8%) of respondents have replied that mobility of industrial waste is extremely inefficient.

Table 4.25: Perceptions for transport system for removal of waste material - Gurugram

N = 260	Gurugram									
	Very efficient		Efficient		Average		Not efficient		Extremely inefficient	
	N	N%	N	N%	N	N%	N	N%	N	N%
Agricultural sources of waste	32	12.3%	122	46.9%	56	21.5%	37	14.2%	13	5.0%

N = 260	Gurugram									
	Very efficient		Efficient		Average		Not efficient		Extremely inefficient	
	N	N%	N	N%	N	N%	N	N%	N	N%
Construction/demolition sources of waste	33	12.7%	69	26.5%	84	32.3%	56	21.5%	18	6.9%
Electronic sources of waste	9	3.5%	82	31.5%	117	45.0%	33	12.7%	19	7.3%
Industrial sources of waste	31	11.9%	82	31.5%	64	24.6%	47	18.1%	36	13.8%
Medical/Clinical sources of waste	68	26.2%	81	31.2%	66	25.4%	34	13.1%	11	4.2%
Municipal sources of waste	38	14.6%	86	33.1%	48	18.5%	78	30.0%	10	3.8%

Perceptions about transport system for removal of waste material – Noida

Table 4.26 shows the perceptions about transport systems for removal of waste material in Noida. In Noida, (44%) respondents have expressed that the transport system is efficient for the removal of agricultural waste, (32%) on municipal waste, (31.4%) on medical/clinical waste and (30%) on industrial sources of waste. As per the table, (24%) of respondents have viewed the transport system to be very efficient for the removal medical/clinical waste, (16%) think the same for municipal waste and (13.1%) for agricultural waste. When it comes to the question of average performance, the data shows that (48.6%) of respondents have replied that the transport system is average for electronic waste, followed by (36.6%) who feel the same for construction/demolition waste, (25.4%) on medical/clinical waste and (24.6%) on industrial waste. When it comes to the question of not efficient or extremely inefficient transport systems, the data explains that (21.9%) of respondents have viewed that the mobility for municipal waste is inefficient, followed by (20.6%) who think the same for construction/demolition waste and (17.0%) about industrial waste. About (16.6%) and (10.9%) of respondents have replied respectively that mobility of industrial waste and construction/demolition waste is extremely inefficient.

Table 4.26: Perceptions for transport system for removal of waste material - Noida

N = 175	Noida									
	Very efficient		Efficient		Average		Not efficient		Extremely inefficient	
	N	N%	N	N%	N	N%	N	N%	N	N%
Agricultural sources of waste	23	13.1%	77	44.0%	44	25.1%	20	11.4%	11	6.3%
Construction/ demolition sources of waste	17	9.7%	39	22.3%	64	36.6%	36	20.6%	19	10.9%
Electronic sources of waste	11	6.3%	46	26.3%	85	48.6%	21	12.0%	12	6.9%
Industrial sources of waste	18	10.3%	54	30.9%	44	25.1%	30	17.1%	29	16.6%
Medical/Clinical sources of waste	42	24.0%	55	31.4%	46	26.3%	23	13.1%	9	5.1%
Municipal sources of waste	28	16.0%	56	32.0%	31	17.7%	51	29.1%	9	5.1%

Perceptions for transport system for removal of waste material - Lucknow

Table 4.27 shows the perception of the transport system for removal of waste material in Lucknow. In Lucknow, (39.5%) of respondents have viewed that the transport system is efficient for the removal of electronic waste, (36.5%) feel it efficient for industrial waste, (36%) for construction/demolition waste and (33.0%) for municipal waste. Here, the data also shows that (26.8%) respondents have said the transport system is very efficient for the removal of industrial waste, (20.3%) think it very efficient for medical/clinical waste and (17.4%) for electronic waste. When it comes to the question of average performance, the data shows that (59.6%) of respondents have viewed it average for agricultural waste, (52.4%) feel the same for medical/clinical waste, (46.4%) for municipal waste and (37%) for construction/demolition waste. When it comes to the question of not efficient or extremely inefficient transport systems, the table indicates that (17.1%) of respondents have said that the mobility for industrial waste is inefficient followed by (16.9%) who think the same for electronic waste and (13.6%) for construction/demolition waste. The table shows that there is a small percentage of respondents who have expressed that the mobility of wastage material in the city is extremely inefficient.

Table 4.27: Perceptions for transport system for removal of waste material - Lucknow

N = 403	Lucknow									
	Very efficient		Efficient		Average		Not efficient		Extremely inefficient	
	N	N%	N	N%	N	N%	N	N%	N	N%
Agricultural sources of waste	53	13.2%	96	23.8%	240	59.6%	14	3.5%	0	0.0%

N = 403	Lucknow									
	Very efficient		**Efficient**		**Average**		**Not efficient**		**Extremely inefficient**	
	N	**N%**	**N**	**N%**	**N**	**N%**	**N**	**N%**	**N**	**N%**
Construction/ demolition sources of waste	41	10.2%	145	36.0%	149	37.0%	55	13.6%	13	3.2%
Electronic sources of waste	70	17.4%	159	39.5%	92	22.8%	68	16.9%	14	3.5%
Industrial sources of waste	108	26.8%	147	36.5%	79	19.6%	69	17.1%	0	0.0%
Medical/ Clinical sources of waste	82	20.3%	96	23.8%	211	52.4%	14	3.5%	0	0.0%
Municipal sources of waste	69	17.1%	133	33.0%	187	46.4%	14	3.5%	0	0.0%

4.14 Priorities that requires immediate attention and in a decade

The term 'priorities' refers to the various opportunities and facilities likely to be available in the city in the short or long period. Facilities like safety, creative and impactful technology, houses, economic opportunities, education for all, quality health services, better transport system and many more are included in the city priorities.

Priorities that require immediate attention

Table 4.28 explains city wise priorities that require immediate attention. The study has covered four cities: Delhi, Gurugram, Noida and Lucknow.

In Delhi, priorities that requires immediate attention are – clean and green city, smart governance, houses, employment and education for all, health facilities for all and smart infrastructure.

In Gurugram, priorities that require immediate attention are – smart governance, clean and green city, health facilities for all, houses, employment and education for all and smart infrastructure.

In Noida, priorities that require immediate attention are – clean and green city, smart governance, houses, employment and education for all, smart infrastructure and health facilities for all.

In Lucknow, priorities that require immediate attention are – health facilities for all, clean and green city, smart governance, smart infrastructure, houses, employment and education for all.

Table 4.28: Priorities that requires immediate attention by region

Priorities	Ranks			
	Delhi	Gurugram	Lucknow	Noida
Clean and Green City	1	2	2	1
Smart Infrastructure	5	5	4	4
Houses, Employment and Education for all	3	4	5	3
Smart Governance	2	1	3	2
Health facilities for all	4	3	1	5

Priorities that requires attention in a decade

Table 4.29 below explains the city wise long-term visions of respondents. The study has covered four cities—Delhi, Gurugram, Lucknow and Noida.

In Delhi, the long-term vision in terms of priorities are – house, employment, education for all, good medical facilities, smart and effective governance and citizen engagement, clean and green city, develop into world class city consisting of smart and efficient services.

In Gurugram, the long-term vision in terms of priorities are – house, employment, education for all, good medical facilities, clean and green city, smart and effective governance and citizen engagement, develop into world class city consisting of smart and efficient services.

In Noida, the long-term vision in terms of priorities are – house, employment, education for all, good medical facilities, smart and effective governance and citizen engagement, clean and green city, develop into world class city consisting of smart and efficient services.

In Lucknow, the long-term vision in terms of priorities are – smart and effective governance and citizen engagement, house, employment, education for all, clean and green city, good medical facilities, develop into world class city consisting of smart and efficient services.

Table 4.29: Priorities that requires attention in a decade

Priorities	Ranks			
	Delhi	Gurugram	Lucknow	Noida
Clean and Green city	4	3	3	4
Develop into world class city consisting of smart and efficient services	5	5	5	5
House, employment, education for all	1	1	2	1

Priorities	Ranks			
	Delhi	Gurugram	Lucknow	Noida
Good medical facilities	2	2	4	2
Smart and effective governance and citizen engagement	3	4	1	3

4.15 Current challenges faced by youth

Table 4.30 highlights the current challenges faced by youth. There are a number of challenges being faced by the youth. A good way to develop a smart city would be to develop infrastructure and facilities to overcome these challenges and provide solutions to problems which respondents value as high priority. Based on the data in Table 4.30, it is evident that respondents are facing many challenges and all cities need to address these challenges at different levels.

Table 4.30: Current challenges faced by youth

Challenges	Delhi N = 1117		Gurugram N = 260		Noida N = 175		Lucknow N = 403	
	N	N%	N	N%	N	N%	N	N%
Decline in Greenery & Cleanliness	879	78.69%	199	76.54%	129	73.71%	376	93.30%
Drop in Cultural values	721	64.55%	171	65.77%	117	66.86%	293	72.70%
Energy efficiency (24*7 Electricity)	557	49.87%	121	46.54%	76	43.43%	175	43.42%
Fall/drop in tourism	522	46.73%	111	42.69%	81	46.29%	281	69.73%

Challenges	Delhi N = 1117		Gurugram N = 260		Noida N = 175		Lucknow N = 403	
	N	N%	N	N%	N	N%	N	N%
Increased crime rates	883	79.05%	206	79.23%	136	77.71%	308	76.43%
Increased Traffic	1052	94.18%	249	95.77%	159	90.86%	349	86.60%
Increasing housing rates	750	67.14%	166	63.85%	117	66.86%	294	72.95%
Infrastructure issues (house, roads)	670	59.98%	151	58.08%	92	52.57%	294	72.95%
Job opportunities and quality	824	73.77%	192	73.85%	120	68.57%	227	56.33%
Lack of Quality of hospitals	666	59.62%	144	55.38%	102	58.29%	282	69.98%
Poor governance	775	69.38%	175	67.31%	116	66.29%	268	66.50%
Poverty	862	77.17%	200	76.92%	129	73.71%	348	86.35%
Rise in pollution	1015	90.87%	235	90.38%	156	89.14%	335	83.13%
Sewerage/Sanitation issues	805	72.07%	186	71.54%	115	65.71%	334	82.88%
Water problems	820	73.41%	187	71.92%	119	68%	107	26.55%

4.16 Perceived improvement of challenges in the next five years

The respondents have expressed their views about perceived improvement in conditions in the next five years. Table 4.31 shows the perceived improvement in conditions in the next five years in surveyed cities. Hence, the table indicates that the major areas that will improve across the cities in the near future are cleanliness and greenery, energy efficiency, infrastructure, sewerage/sanitation issues, traffic, crime rates. These areas need to be addressed by the concerned authorities.

Table 4.31: Perceived improvement of challenges in next five years

	Delhi N = 1117			Gurugram N = 260			Noida N = 175			Lucknow N = 403		
	Will Im-prove	Will De-crease	Will get worse	Will Im-prove	Will De-crease	Will get worse	Will Im-prove	Will De-crease	Will get worse	Will Im-prove	Will De-crease	Will get worse
Crime rates	45.33%	38.50%	16.10%	42.86%	41.36%	15.79%	42.45%	41.33%	15.64%	13.58%	66.95%	19.89%
Energy efficiency (24★7 Electricity)	76.66%	13.30%	9.98%	75.94%	11.28%	12.03%	78.20%	14.52%	7.82%	79.56%	16.98%	3.40%
Greenery & Cleanliness	79.29%	16.10%	4.55%	81.96%	16.54%	2.26%	82.67%	12.29%	5.59%	79.56%	16.98%	3.40%
Housing rates	47.43%	32.38%	20.30%	42.86%	35.34%	21.81%	43.57%	31.28%	25.69%	47.06%	33.47%	19.40%
Infrastructure issues (house, roads)	46.73%	50.23%	2.98%	43.61%	54.14%	1.50%	43.57%	53.62%	3.35%	77.13%	23.29%	0%
Job opportunities and quality	33.95%	51.11%	14.88%	27.82%	57.15%	15.04%	29.05%	52.51%	18.99%	69.86%	19.89%	10.19%
Pollution Level	57.58%	28.35%	14%	56.39%	30.08%	13.53%	54.74%	26.81%	17.87%	20.37%	43.17%	36.38%

	Delhi N = 1117			Gurugram N = 260			Noida N = 175			Lucknow N = 403		
	Will Improve	Will Decrease	Will get worse	Will Improve	Will Decrease	Will get worse	Will Improve	Will Decrease	Will get worse	Will Improve	Will Decrease	Will get worse
Poor governance	52.51%	33.25%	14.18%	51.13%	36.09%	13.53%	53.62%	30.16%	16.76%	43.66%	40.26%	16.49%
Poverty	81.04%	12.25%	6.65%	81.21%	11.28%	6.77%	81.55%	11.17%	7.82%	36.38%	60.15%	3.40%
Quality of hospitals	57.41%	31.68%	10.85%	53.39%	34.59%	12.03%	52.51%	34.63%	13.41%	66.95%	33.47%	0%
Sewerage/ Sanitation issues	54.08%	34.65%	11.20%	52.63%	36.09%	12.03%	51.39%	34.63%	14.52%	66.95%	33.47%	0%
Tourism Footfall	56.36%	41.83%	1.75%	52.63%	45.87%	1.50%	54.74%	42.45%	3.35%	47.06%	46.57%	6.79%
Traffic	64.41%	34.83%	0.70%	61.66%	38.35%	0%	62.56%	36.87%	0%	10.19%	62.58%	27.17%
Water Availability	40.26%	31.50%	28.18%	37.60%	32.33%	29.33%	39.10%	29.05%	32.40%	47.06%	42.69%	9.70%

4.17 Prioritization of features in making the surveyed city as a smart city

The respondents have expressed their views in Table 4.32 about prioritization of features in making their city into a smart city. The respondents in Delhi have indicated that the high priority areas are health (47%), education (51.7%), water supply (48.7%), energy supply (43.3%), safety and security (48.9%), waste water management (46.9%) and air quality (46.8%) followed by other challenges highlighted in the table. Similarly, for respondents in Gurugram the high priority areas are heath (11%), education (12.1%), economy and employment (9.9%), water supply (11.3%), energy supply (10.1%), safety and security (11.4%), waste water management (11%) and air quality (10.8%).

In Noida, the respondents have prioritized on safety and security (7.7%), water supply (7.8%), waste water management (7.4%) and health (7.4%). It can be concluded from the analysis that safety and security, health, education, water supply and energy supply are priorities in all cities.

For respondents in Lucknow, the major challenges with high priority are health (16.7%), education (16.5%), economy and employment (16.3%), transportation (16.5%), water supply (19.2%) energy supply (17.1%), safety and security (18.5%), water management (16.4%) air quality (17.1%) and underground electric wiring and sanitation (16.4%). The table shows that there are a number of challenges faced by the respondents of Lucknow but the major ones are safety, security and air quality.

Table 4.32: Prioritization of features in making Delhi a smart city by region

High Priority for various Indicators	Delhi N = 1117 High Priority	Gurugram N = 260 High Priority	Noida N = 175 High Priority	Lucknow N = 403 High Priority
Air Quality	46.8%	10.8%	7.3%	17.1%
Citizen Engagement	20.7%	4.3%	3.2%	14.9%
City Identity and Culture	24.2%	5.3%	4.0%	14.4%
Compact City	18.7%	4.1%	2.5%	12.4%
Economy and Employment	42.2%	9.9%	6.3%	16.3%
Education	51.7%	12.1%	8.1%	16.5%
Energy Efficiency	35.0%	7.9%	5.5%	11.6%
Energy Supply	43.3%	10.1%	6.7%	17.1%
Health	47.0%	11.0%	7.4%	16.7%
Housing and Inclusiveness	19.7%	4.4%	2.8%	12.9%
Intelligent Govt. Services	38.0%	8.8%	5.9%	14.3%
IT connectivity	28.7%	6.6%	4.2%	15.4%
Public Open Spaces	21.4%	4.5%	3.2%	9.7%
Safety and Security	48.9%	11.4%	7.7%	18.5%
Sanitation	33.4%	7.5%	4.8%	16.4%
Transportation	29.6%	6.7%	4.5%	16.5%
Underground Electric Wiring	21.9%	4.7%	3.4%	16.4%
Walkable	28.3%	6.6%	4.2%	12.4%

High Priority for various Indicators	Delhi N = 1117	Gurugram N = 260	Noida N = 175	Lucknow N = 403
	High Priority	High Priority	High Priority	High Priority
Waste Water Management	46.9%	11.0%	7.4%	13.1%
Water Management	41.9%	9.8%	6.4%	16.4%
Water Supply	48.7%	11.3%	7.8%	15.0%

To understand more about perceptions, the data was analyzed for males and females. Next chapter highlights the regional differences in perceptions.

Chapter 5
Perceptions based on Gender

This chapter highlights the gender perceptions of respondents in mobility-related areas such as commuting time, money involved in commuting, consumer's satisfaction level with time and money involved, existing problems with public transport system and their safety, their perceptions for services which are likely to improve in the near future and their expectation from Government and policymakers to encourage green transport in their cities. It also highlights the policy measures that should be initiated/strengthened to improve the urban transport system. The data was analyzed for Delhi, Gurugram, Noida and Lucknow.

Perceptions related to green transport were also recorded to know the current efforts made by respondents. Questions relating to mobility of goods and transport system for removal of waste material were also recorded. Respondents also shared their views about priorities that require immediate attention and in a decade for their cities. This chapter also highlights the current challenges faced by respondents in their cities and perceived improvement approaches for the next five years.

5.1 Transport mode used by the respondents

Transport used by male respondents

Table 5.1 indicates the gender wise frequency for using various transport modes in Delhi. Here, the transport modes are classified into six categories i.e. bus, metro, e-rickshaw, scooter, car and auto which are being used by male and female respondents in surveyed cities. The data shows that the male respondents use all type of transport modes. A significant percentage of male respondents (16.4%) do not use the metro. These responses are from Lucknow as at the time of survey the metro was not operational in the city. Scooter is also another mode of transport which is used once every few months. Perhaps, pollution and safety are the reasons for not using two-wheelers in the surveyed cities. Bus, metro and shared autos are used more than five days a week.

Table 5.1: Transport mode used by the respondents

N = 1082	Male											
	5+ days a week		2-4 days a week		Once a week		Once a month		More than in a month		Not at all	
	N	N%	N	N%	N	N%	N	N%	N	N%	N	N%
Auto	195	18.0%	352	32.5%	71	6.6%	248	22.9%	190	17.6%	26	2.4%
Bus	349	32.3%	230	21.3%	147	13.6%	121	11.2%	193	17.8%	42	3.9%
Car	249	23.0%	165	15.2%	129	11.9%	222	20.5%	289	26.7%	28	2.6%
E-rickshaw	244	22.6%	128	11.8%	251	23.2%	289	26.7%	156	14.4%	14	1.3%
Metro	304	28.1%	345	31.9%	103	9.5%	37	3.4%	116	10.7%	177	16.4%
Scooter	144	13.3%	127	11.7%	99	9.1%	186	17.2%	471	43.5%	55	5.1%
Shared Auto	313	28.9%	215	19.9%	175	16.2%	183	16.9%	169	15.62%	27	2.5%

Transport use by female respondents

Table 5.2 represents the female view on frequency of using various transport modes in surveyed cities. The data shows that the female respondents prefer metro followed by auto, scooter and shared auto for five working days of the week.

Table 5.2: *Transport mode used by the respondents*

	Female											
	5+ days a week		2-4 days a week		Once a week		Once a month		More than in a month		Not at all	
	N	N%	N	N%	N	N%	N	N%	N	N%	N	N%
Auto★	196	22.8%	275	32.0%	92	10.7%	62	7.2%	169	19.7%	66	7.7%
Bus★★	153	17.5%	254	29.1%	134	15.3%	167	19.1%	139	15.9%	26	3.0%
Car★	167	19.4%	301	35.0%	98	11.4%	71	8.3%	157	18.3%	66	7.7%
E-rick-shaw★★	141	16.2%	84	9.6%	141	16.2%	258	29.6%	249	28.5%	0	0.0%
Metro★	224	26.0%	133	15.5%	127	14.8%	56	6.5%	96	11.2%	224	26.0%
Scooter★	179	20.8%	282	32.8%	102	11.9%	35	4.1%	210	24.4%	52	6.0%
Shared Auto★★	180	20.6%	231	26.5%	135	15.5%	219	25.1%	108	12.4%	0	0.0%

★N = 860, ★★ N = 873

5.2 Factors related to mobility

Monthly expenditure on mobility

Table 5.3 explains gender wise monthly expenditure on mobility. It highlights that there is no significant difference among travel costs irrespective of respondent's gender. Both the genders spend a maximum amount between ₹1001-₹3000.

Table 5.3: Monthly expenditure on mobility in ₹

	Male, N = 1082		Female, N = 873	
	N	N%	N	N%
Less than 1000	278	25.7%	224	25.7%
Between 1001–3000	479	44.3%	375	43.0%
Between 3001–5000	158	14.6%	135	15.5%
Above 5000	167	15.4%	139	15.9%

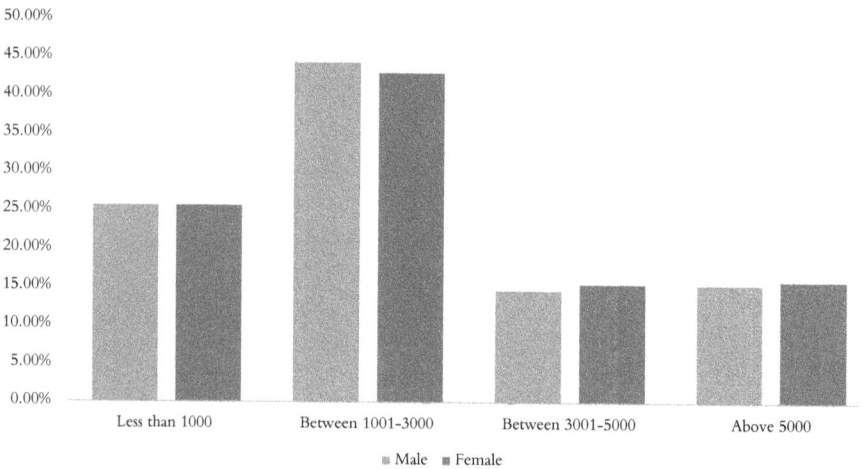

Figure 5.1: Monthly expenditure on mobility in ₹

Cost of mobility in next few years

Table 5.4 highlights the perceptions about increase in the monthly cost of mobility. (68.8%) male respondents agreed that the cost will increase in future and (24.2%) said they strongly agree that the cost will increase in the future.

Whereas, very few male respondents, (3.6%) and (3.4%) respectively, strongly disagreed and disagreed with opinions regarding the increase in cost of mobility.

Similarly, (67.1%) female respondents agreed and (20.7%) said they strongly agreed that the cost will increase in the future. Only (12.1%) female respondents have disagreed with the thought of an increase in mobility cost. Both male and female respondents also expressed that insufficient public transport facility is one of the key causes for an increase in cost of mobility.

Table 5.4: Cost of mobility in near future will increase over time

	Male, N = 1082		Female, N = 873	
	N	N%	N	N%
Strongly Agree	262	24.2%	181	20.7%
Agree	744	68.8%	586	67.1%
Disagree	37	3.4%	106	12.1%
Strongly Disagree	39	3.6%	0	0.0%

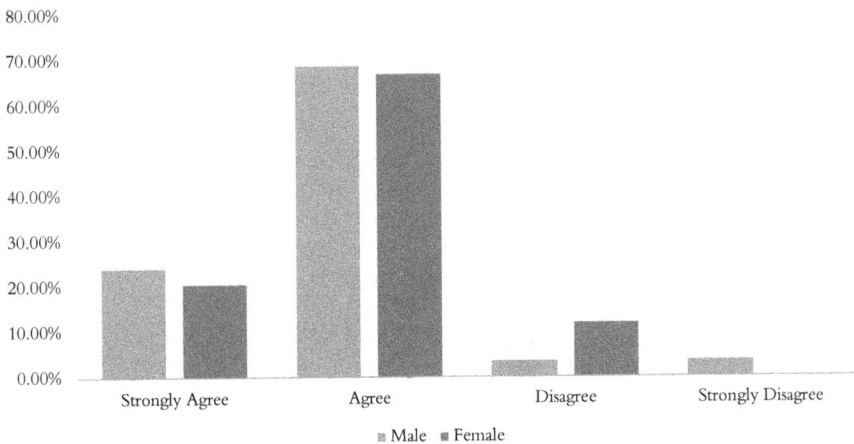

Figure 5.2: Cost of mobility in near future will increase over time

Satisfaction level on money and spent on travel

Table 5.5 explains the gender wise level of satisfaction of respondents in relation to their monthly expenditure on mobility. There is a significant difference between satisfaction levels of male and female respondents. (40.39%) of the male respondents are satisfied with time and money spent on travel, on the other hand, only (35%) of the female respondents are satisfied with the time and money spent.

The data also concludes that there is a significant percentage of female respondents who are dissatisfied with their current expenditure on mobility in comparison to male respondents.

Table 5.5: Satisfied with the time and money spend

	Male, N = 1082		Female, N = 873	
	N	N%	N	N%
Very satisfied	114	10.5%	110	12.6%
Satisfied	437	40.3%	306	35%
Neither	257	23.7%	195	22.3%
Dissatisfied	199	18.3%	219	25%
Very dissatisfied	75	6.9%	43	4.9%

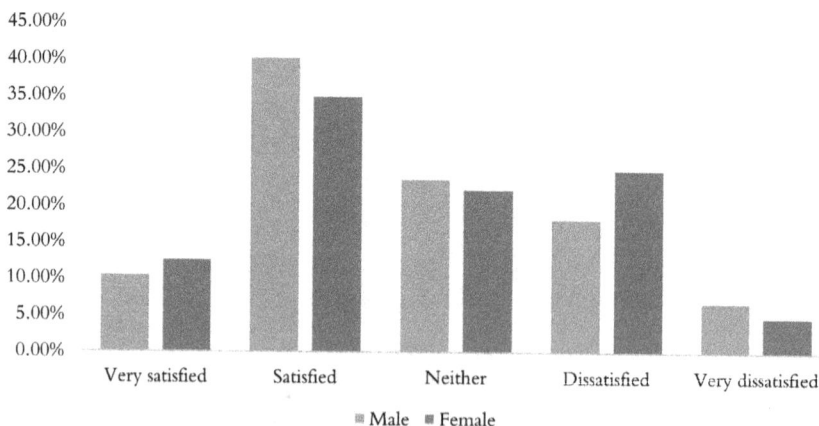

Figure 5.3: Satisfaction level with time and money spent

5.3 Problems with public transport

Table 5.6 shows the problems faced by both genders while using public transportation in four cities under study. Out of the total male respondents, (87.2%) said that the problem is related to waiting period which is too long for preferred route, (86%) feel that non-reliability, especially during non-peak hours is the main problem, (79.5%) male respondents said that last mile connectivity is not available, about (76.5%) said that public transportation does not ensure safety of personal belongings, (73.2%) respondents believe that public vehicles are over-crowded. At the same time, about (26.8%) of male respondents said that carrying their belongings in public transport is not a problem, (26.8%) feel that public transportation not over-crowded and according to (20.5%) male respondents, availability of last mile connectivity is not an issue. Few male respondents do not find waiting period reliability, especially during non-peak hours, a major problem.

Out of the total female respondents, (75%) feel that reliability of public transport especially during non-peak hours is a major issue, (71.6%) said that the problem is related to waiting period which is too long for preferred route, (71.4%) female respondents find public transports over-crowded, about (67.4%) said that public transportation does not ensure safety of personal belongings and (58.6%) females said that last mile connectivity is not available. At the same time, about (41.4%) female respondents do not find last mile connectivity a major issue, (32.6%) of females do not find public transport unsafe for carrying personal belongings and as per (28.4%) of female respondents waiting period is not an issue.

Table 5.6: Problems with public transport

	Male, N = 1082				Female, N = 873			
	Yes		No		Yes		No	
	N	N%	N	N%	N	N%	N	N%
Last mile connectivity is not available	860	79.5%	222	20.5%	512	58.6%	361	41.4%
Not reliable specially during non-peak hours	930	86.0%	152	14.0%	655	75.0%	218	25.0%
Not safe for carrying the belongings	828	76.5%	254	23.5%	588	67.4%	285	32.6%
Over – crowded	792	73.2%	290	26.8%	623	71.4%	250	28.6%
Waiting period is too long for preferred route	944	87.2%	138	12.8%	625	71.6%	248	28.4%

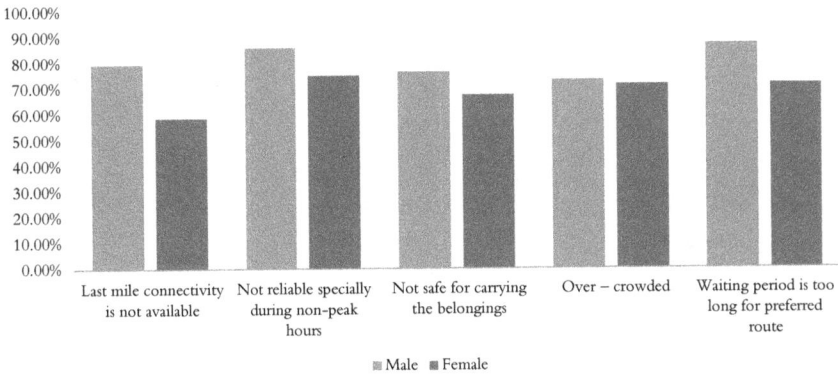

Figure 5.4: Problems with public transport

5.4 Personal safety in public transport

Respondents were asked about their personal safety while travelling by public transport and had five options to rate their views as mentioned in Table 5.7. The data shows that there is significant difference in opinion among male and female respondents. It can be derived from the study that personal safety during travelling for women is a concern because many of them rated the current mode of public transport as poor and inadequate.

Table 5.7: Personal safety in public transport

	Male, N = 1082		Female, N = 873	
	N	N%	N	N%
Very good	147	13.6%	77	8.8%
Good	273	25.2%	249	28.5%
Average	422	39.0%	312	35.7%
Poor	149	13.8%	149	17.1%
Very Poor	91	8.4%	86	9.9%

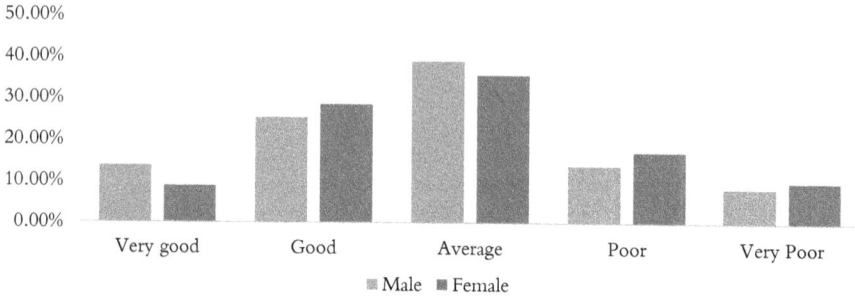

Figure 5.5: Personal Safety in Public Transport

5.5 Services that may improve in next five years

Table 5.8 shows gender wise views of respondents related to the services that will improve in next five years. There are various services categorically mentioned here and each service has its own significance to develop a world class smart city. Respondents were given four choices to rate services that will improve in next five years. These options were improvement to a great extent, somewhat, very little and not at all.

From the total male respondents, (46.2%) male viewed that there would be improvement in bicycle rental and mobility infrastructure to a great extent, (44.4%) said parking management and (42.9%) viewed that traffic management will improve to a great extent, (25.6%) feel the same about management of means of transport. Similarly, (67.4%) male respondents feel that there would be somewhat improvement on car share platform, (53.8%) feel the same about traceability and logistics applications and (50.8%) feel it about management of means of transport. The study also indicates that (42.5%) of males expressed that there will be little improvement on charging points for electric cars, (50.8%) said the same about bicycle rental and mobility infrastructure, (26.5%) feel it about traceability and logistics applications. The study also reveals that there is a small percentage of male respondents who replied that there will be no improvement at all in certain areas like traffic management (14.4%) and charging points for electric cars (9.1%).

The view of female respondents in same areas is as follows: (41.2%) female respondents said that there will be an improvement in traffic management (Detector of free parking places) to a great extent, (38.1%) feel the same about management of means of transport, (36%) female respondents viewed that traffic management will improve to a great extent and (23.1%) feel the same about bicycle rental and mobility infrastructure. Similarly, (67.2%) female respondents think that there will be somewhat improvement in traceability and logistics applications, (66.1%) female respondents feel the same about car share platform and (46%) on charging points for electric cars. (37.6%) of females expressed that there will be little improvement on bicycle rental and mobility infrastructure and (31.4%) feel the same about charging points for electric cars. The table also shows that there is a small percentage of female respondents who viewed that there will be no improvement at all in certain areas like traffic management (11.8%) and charging points for electric cars (8.2%). So, it can be said from the table that majority of respondents have agreed that there would be an improvement in the services of car share platform, traceability and logistic applications, traffic management, bicycle rental and mobility infrastructure.

Table 5.8: Services that may improve in next five years

	Male, N = 1082				Female, N = 873			
	To a Great Extent	Some-what	Very Little	Not at All	To a Great Extent	Some-what	Very Little	Not at All
Bicycle rental and mobility infrastructure	46.2%	17.5%	30.1%	6.2%	23.1%	31.0%	37.6%	8.2%
Car-share plat-form	22.9%	67.4%	8.4%	1.3%	22.8%	66.1%	7.9%	3.2%
Charging points for electric cars	15.9%	32.4%	42.5%	9.1%	14.3%	46.0%	31.4%	8.2%
Management of means of trans-port	25.6%	50.8%	18.9%	4.6%	38.1%	42.3%	16.6%	3.0%
Parking manage-ment	44.4%	33.2%	15.6%	6.8%	36.0%	32.3%	27.9%	3.8%
Traceability and logistics applica-tions	17.6%	53.8%	26.5%	2.1%	20.5%	67.2%	10.1%	2.2%
Traffic manage-ment (Detector of free parking places)	42.9%	25.9%	16.8%	14.4%	41.2%	33.8%	13.2%	11.8%

5.6 Services may improve in near future

Table 5.9 shows the different kinds of transport systems and gender wise views of respondents regarding the transportation system and its improvement in a future smart city. The study highlights that male respondents expect public transport to be better in the future whereas the percentage of female responses is higher for shared transport. There is no significant difference between responses of male and female respondents for private transport. So, in order to meet the needs of people the state governments should emphasize more on public transport as it caters to the transportation needs of a larger population, who basically belong to middle income or lower income groups. The government should also come up with new plans and strategies to make public transportation more convenient.

Table 5.9: Services which may improve in near future

	Male, N = 1082		Female, N = 873	
	N	N%	N	N%
Public transport	652	60.3%	478	54.8%
Private transport	113	10.4%	85	9.7%
Shared transport	317	29.3%	310	35.5%

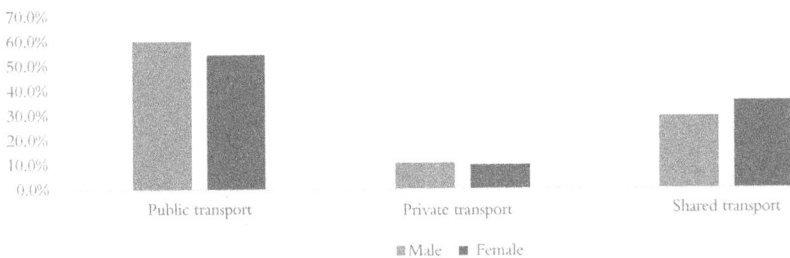

■ Male ■ Female

Figure 5.6: Services which may improve in near future

5.7 Transport mode that may improve in next five years

Table *5.10* shows the gender wise views on what is expected to be better for personal transport. Both male and female respondents shared that metro is going to be better in next five years and will provide them better connectivity. Only (6.41%) of female respondents shared that bus services may improve in next five years in surveyed cities.

Table 5.10: Transport mode that may improve in next five years

	Male, N = 1082		Female, N = 873	
	N	N%	N	N%
Buses	208	19.22%	56	6.41%
Trains like Metro	568	52.50%	495	56.70%
Good roads	230	21.26%	254	29.10%
Private Autos	76	7.02%	68	7.79%

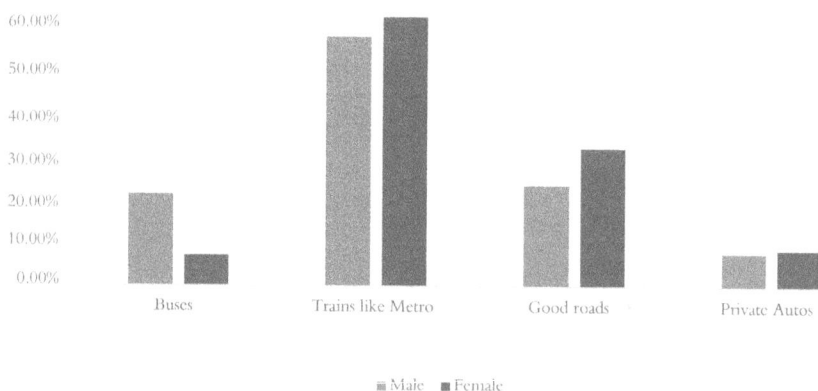

Figure 5.7: Transport mode that may improve in next five years

5.8 Willingness to pay additional money for better transport

Government of India defines the income level[1] for Other Backward Classes (OBCs) time to time, for example, the limit was ₹1 lakh per year in 1993, ₹2.4 lakh per year in 2004, ₹4.5 lakh per year in 2008, ₹6 lakh in 2013 and ₹8 lakh in 2017. *Table 5.11* explains the gender wise views on willingness to pay additional money to have better public transport. The data highlights that there is significant difference between males and females for the amount of less than ₹1000 and above ₹5000. The least difference among male and female respondents is for the amount of ₹3001 – ₹5000. The data also highlights that female respondents are willing to pay more money for better transport and the additional amount is between ₹1001 – ₹3000.

Table 5.11: Willing to pay additional money for better transport

Amount in ₹	Male, N = 1082		Female, N = 873	
	N	N%	N	N%
Less than 1000	495	45.7%	303	34.7%
Between 1001–3000	381	35.2%	346	39.6%
Between 3001–5000	140	12.9%	101	11.6%
Above 5000	66	6.1%	123	14.1%

---

1   This helps in identifying the relatively forward and better educated members of the OBCs who are not eligible for availing the government-sponsored educational and professional benefit programs.

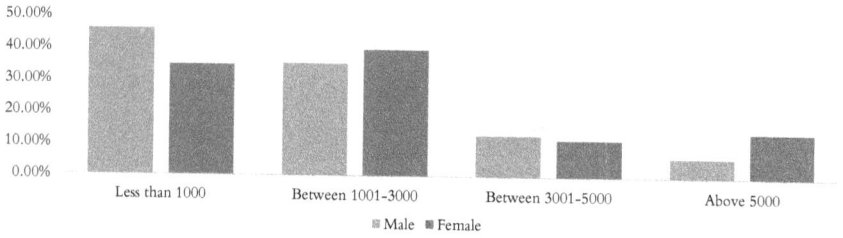

Figure 5.8: Willing to pay additional money for better transport (amount in ₹)

5.9 Suggested measures to promote green transport

Table 5.12 highlights the gender wise views of respondents on policies for green transport. The data reveals that (93.9%) of male respondents have given a higher priority to building road networks to support green transport, (88.7%) have given a higher priority on ensuring sufficient supply of electricity for each family, (88.6%) on providing subsidy to manufacturers and (88.2%) on infrastructural support by installing charging stations. The table also shows that (60.2%) of male respondents think that providing subsidies to consumers is a secondary priority in comparison to other policies. Out of the total male respondents, (39.8%) said green transport cannot be promoted by providing subsidies to consumers, (11.8%) do not agree with the idea of infrastructural support by installing charging stations and (11.4%) do not believe that green transport can be achieved by providing subsidies to manufacturers.

In case of female respondents, (86.0%) give more priority to infrastructural support by installing charging stations, (84.8%) support ensuring sufficient supply of electricity for each family, (83.2%) go with building road networks to support green transport and (75%) support providing subsidies to manufacturers. (46.8%) think that providing subsidies to consumers will support green transport. At the same time, (53.2%) female respondents think that green transport cannot be promoted by providing subsidies to consumers, (25%) do not support providing subsidies to manufacturers and (16.8%) do not believe that building road networks will support green transport. It can be concluded from the study that the government needs to build road networks, infrastructure support and supply of sufficient electricity for each family in order to support green transport systems which are crucial for developing a future smart city.

Table 5.12: Suggested measures to promote green transport

	Male, N = 1082				Female, N = 873			
	Yes		No		Yes		No	
	N	N%	N	N%	N	N%	N	N%
By building road network to support the Green Transport	1016	93.9%	66	6.1%	726	83.2%	147	16.8%
By providing subsidy to consumers	651	60.2%	431	39.8%	409	46.8%	464	53.2%
By providing subsidy to manufacturers	959	88.6%	123	11.4%	655	75.0%	218	25.0%
Ensuring sufficient supply of electricity for each family	960	88.7%	122	11.3%	740	84.8%	133	15.2%
Through infrastructural support by installing charging stations	954	88.2%	128	11.8%	751	86.0%	122	14.0%

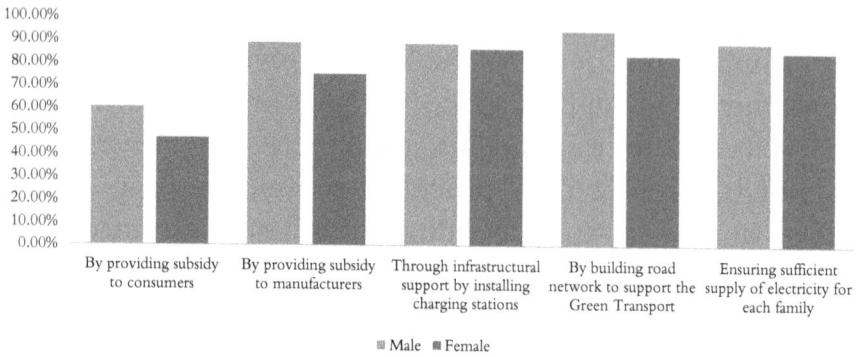

Figure 5.9: Suggested measures to promote green transport

5.10 Measures for improvement in urban transport system

Table 5.13 explains the gender wise views of respondents on measures for urban transportation. The table shows that all services mentioned are crucial to develop a smart city particularly in the area of transportation. The eight measures which are mentioned in the table are equally important for respondents to build a sound transport system and they believe that the areas under study are not adequately equipped with these measures. The table shows (92%) of male respondents said enhancing transport coordination through real time updates is a key measure for better urban transport. (91.7%) support promoting car sharing/pooling, (90.2%) agreed to focus upon public transport particularly bus transport and (89.7%) said compliance for vehicle emission standards and inspection and maintenance is important. Similarly, there is a significant percentage of male respondents who also emphasized on other services mentioned in the table. Out of the total male respondents about (12.3%) of respondents said that they do not find introducing a variety of bus transport services should be a priority, (11.9%) of respondents do not find encouraging green modes/transports important and (11.8%) think that improving the efficiency of bus transport operation is not necessary for urban transport.

Similarly, in case of female respondents, (86.3%) of them agreed on restraining the use of polluting vehicles and fuels, (85.6%) agreed on promoting car sharing/pooling, (77.2%) support encouraging green modes/transports and (76.9%) support compliance for vehicle emission standards and inspection and maintenance. There is also a significant percentage of female respondents who emphasized on other services, which are given in the table. Out of the total female respondents, about (29.3%) of them do not agree on focusing on public transport, particularly bus transport, (26.8%) do not support introducing a variety of bus transport services and (25.2%) do not find improving the efficiency of bus transport operation as a viable option. Large scale migration leads to limited availability of transport system and in order to provide a good transport system, the respective governments have to take all the initiatives that promote the public transport system.

Table 5.13: Measures for improvement in urban transport system

	Male, N = 1082				Female, N = 873			
	Yes		No		Yes		No	
	N	N%	N	N%	N	N%	N	N%
Compliance for vehicle emission standards and inspection and maintenance	971	89.7%	111	10.3%	671	76.9%	202	23.1%
Encouraging green modes/ transports	953	88.1%	129	11.9%	674	77.2%	199	22.8%
Enhancing transport coordination through real time update	995	92.0%	87	8.0%	671	76.9%	202	23.1%

	Male, N = 1082				Female, N = 873			
	Yes		No		Yes		No	
	N	N%	N	N%	N	N%	N	N%
Focusing on public transport particularly bus transport	976	90.2%	106	9.8%	617	70.7%	256	29.3%
Improving the efficiency of bus transport operation	954	88.2%	128	11.8%	653	74.8%	220	25.2%
Introducing variety of bus transport ser-vices	949	87.7%	133	12.3%	639	73.2%	234	26.8%
Promoting car sharing/pooling	992	91.7%	90	8.3%	747	85.6%	126	14.4%
Restraining the use of polluting vehicles and fuels	963	89.0%	119	11.0%	753	86.3%	120	13.7%

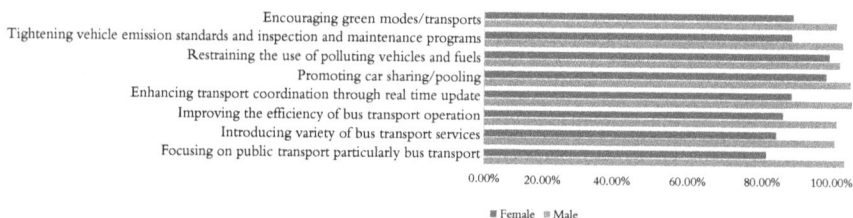

Figure 5.10: Measures for improvement in urban transport system

5.11 Perceptions for green transport

Perception of male respondents

Table 5.14 explains the perceptions of respondents for green transport. The male respondents have different views on the use of transportation and its impact on the environment. (37.6%) of male respondents have strongly agreed with the option that they are currently trying their best to reduce car use. (36.7%) support the view that using public transportation rather than a car helps preserve the environment, (34.9%) strongly agree that more than half of the vehicles in India will be replaced by electric vehicles in 20 years, (33.8%) support the view that public transport is easy to use and (28.1%) believe that the network of charging modes is a prerequisite for the use of green transport. Similarly, there are other points such as high cost of green transport, personal automobiles represent status in society to which many respondents have strongly agreed.

(45%) of male respondents have agreed on the view that using public transportation rather than a car helps preserve the environment, (43.6%) agree that a network of charging modes is a prerequisite for the use of green transport, (37.4%) agree with the point that there will be a fall in green transport prices in the near future and (26.1%) of respondents has agreed that public transport is easy to use.

(49.3%) of respondents are neutral on the point that green transport is expensive, (33.1%) are neutral regarding the need to reduce car use, (30.8%) are neutral regarding the statement that there will be a fall in green transport prices in the near future and (27.0%) of them are neutral regarding the point that an automobile is a necessity for them. There are also other points mentioned in the table.

The data also indicates that about (20%) of male respondents have disagreed that automobiles represent status in society. (18.5%) disagree that an automobile is a necessity for them and (9.8%) disagree that a network of charging modes is a prerequisite for the use of green transport. About (13.9%) of respondents strongly disagree that an automobile is a necessity for them.

Table 5.14: Perceptions for green transport

N = 1082	Male									
	Strongly Agree		Agree		Neutral		Disagree		Strongly Disagree	
	N	N%	N	N%	N	N%	N	N%	N	N%
A network of charging mode is a prereq-uisite for the use of Green Transport	304	28.1%	472	43.6%	184	17.0%	106	9.8%	16	1.5%
An automobile is a necessity for me.	203	18.8%	237	21.9%	292	27.0%	200	18.5%	150	13.9%
Green trans-ports are expensive.	118	10.9%	324	29.9%	533	49.3%	72	6.7%	35	3.2%
I am currently trying my best to reduce car use	407	37.6%	279	25.8%	285	26.3%	83	7.7%	28	2.6%
More than half of vehicles in India will be replaced by Electric vehicle in 20 years	378	34.9%	326	30.1%	213	19.7%	143	13.2%	22	2.0%
Personal Automobiles represent status in society.	266	24.6%	351	32.4%	207	19.1%	216	20.0%	42	3.9%

N = 1082	Male									
	Strongly Agree		Agree		Neutral		Disagree		Strongly Disagree	
	N	N%	N	N%	N	N%	N	N%	N	N%
Public transport is and 9.8% easy to use.	366	33.8%	391	36.1%	228	21.1%	83	7.7%	14	1.3%
There is no need to reduce car use if I own a Green transport.	193	17.8%	307	28.4%	358	33.1%	201	18.6%	23	2.1%
There will be a fall in green transport prices in the near future.	133	12.3%	405	37.4%	333	30.8%	127	11.7%	84	7.8%
Using public transportation other than a car helps preserve the environment	397	36.7%	492	45.5%	33	3.0%	159	14.7%	1	.1%

Perception of female respondents

Table 5.15 shows the perceptions of female respondents for green transport. Out of the total female respondents, (47.1%) have strongly agreed with the option that more than half of the vehicles in India will be replaced by electric vehicles in 20 years, (29%) strongly agree that there is no need to reduce car use if they own a green transport, (28.7%) strongly agree that they are currently trying their best to reduce car use, (27%) go with the point that automobiles represent status in society, (26.3%) feel that a network of charging modes is a prerequisite for the use of green transport. Similarly, there are other areas such as an automobile is a necessity, where respondents strongly agree.

Similarly there are (62.1%) female respondents who agreed that using public transportation rather than a car helps preserve the environment, (41.7%) agreed that there is no need to reduce car use if they own a green transport and (34.9%) of respondents have said public transport is easy to use.

While it comes to the issue of being neutral, (43.5%) of the respondents shared that green transport is expensive, (41.2%) are neutral regarding a network of charging modes as a prerequisite for the use of green transport, (27.5%) remained neutral on the statement that an automobile is a necessity for them and (23.1%) remained neutral with the point that more than half of vehicles in India will be replaced by electric vehicles in 20 years.

The table also shows that about (24.7%) of female respondents disagree that there will be a reduction in green transport prices in near future, (16%) disagree that there is no need to reduce car use if they own a green transport and (14.1%) disagree that they are currently trying their best to reduce car use. There are few respondents who strongly disagree with their perceptions for automobile and green transport.

Table 5.15: Perception on green transport

N = 873	Female									
	Strongly Agree		Agree		Neutral		Disagree		Strongly Disagree	
	N	N%	N	N%	N	N%	N	N%	N	N%
A network of charging mode is a prerequisite for the use of Green Transport	230	26.3%	224	25.7%	360	41.2%	59	6.8%	0	0.0%
An automobile is a necessity for me.	232	26.6%	287	32.9%	240	27.5%	70	8.0%	44	5.0%
Personal automobiles represent status in society.	236	27.0%	297	34.0%	170	19.5%	106	12.1%	64	7.3%
Green transports are expensive.	94	10.8%	286	32.8%	380	43.5%	47	5.4%	66	7.6%
I am currently trying my best to reduce car use	247	28.7%	270	31.4%	208	24.2%	121	14.1%	14	1.6%
More than half of vehicles in India will be replaced by Electric Vehicle in 20 years	411	47.1%	184	21.1%	202	23.1%	73	8.4%	3	.3%
Public transport is easy to use.	221	25.3%	305	34.9%	271	31.0%	50	5.7%	26	3.0%

N = 873	Female									
	Strongly Agree		Agree		Neutral		Disagree		Strongly Disagree	
	N	N%	N	N%	N	N%	N	N%	N	N%
There is no need to reduce car use if I own a Green transport.	253	29.0%	364	41.7%	94	10.8%	140	16.0%	22	2.5%
There will be a fall in green transport prices in the near future.	128	14.7%	362	41.5%	135	15.5%	216	24.7%	32	3.7%
Using public transportation other than a car helps preserve the environment	162	18.6%	542	62.1%	61	7.0%	108	12.4%	0	0.0%

5.12 Perceptions of efficiency in mobility of goods

Table *5.16* shows that both female and male respondents have agreed that the current goods mobility is not very efficient. They pointed out that the mobility of manufactured goods, construction material, packers and movers and water supply is not very efficient as compared to other goods vehicles. They have also viewed that vehicles for food items, fruits and vegetables is efficient because it provides necessary food items on everyday basis to the millions of people in the city. Both male and female have viewed that efficiency for manufactured goods, packers and movers and construction material is good because the city has been witnessing a large number of development projects and construction of infrastructure from last few years. The data also shows that the water supply is big concern for female respondents as the city is unable to provide an adequate amount of water on a daily basis. The female participants have said that most villages on the outskirts of Delhi-NCR and Lucknow have no piped connections and various localities depend on tankers provided by the Delhi Jal Board[2] (DJB) and Lucknow Jal Sansthan. The number of water supply tankers is small in number and has failed to supply adequate water to various localities. A small percentage of respondents says that the mobility of above mentioned items are extremely inefficient.

Views of male respondents

Table 5.16 indicates the male respondents' perception for efficiency related to the mobility of goods. Here, the mobility of vehicles was classified into six categories. These categories are

- Construction material
- Food items
- Fruits and Vegetables
- Manufactured goods
- Packer and Movers
- Supply of water

Here, the data shows there is a small percentage of respondents who have agreed that mobility of goods in the categories are strongly efficient. The data indicate that only (28.5%) of respondents have agreed that the mobility of foods and vegetables is very efficient, (20%) feel the same about food items and (13.7%) about construction material. However, there is a significant percentage of male respondents who agree that mobility of goods is efficient. For instance, the data reveals that (54.4%) of

---

2 Delhi Jal Board is the government agency responsible for supply of potable water to the most of the National Capital Territory region of Delhi, India.

respondents have viewed the mobility of food items as efficient, (50%) think the same about manufactured goods, (49.8%) about fruits and vegetables and (45.7%) about construction material. Many of the respondents have also expressed that the mobility of goods is average. For instance, (37.2%) of respondents said mobility for water supply is Average, (35.9%) think the same about packers and movers, (33.5%) about construction material and (30.1%) about manufactured goods. Similarly, (11.9%) of respondents have said that water supply is not efficient, (9.7%) said the same about fruits and vegetables and (7.3%) about food items. When it comes to the question of extremely inefficient services, (6.5%) male respondent agreed that mobility of food items is extremely inefficient and (4.6%) shared that the mobility of packers and movers is also extremely inefficient.

Table 5.16: Male perceptions of efficiency in mobility of goods

N = 1082	Male									
	Very efficient		Efficient		Average		Not efficient		Extremely inefficient	
	N	N%	N	N%	N	N%	N	N%	N	N%
Construction material	148	13.7%	495	45.7%	362	33.5%	76	7.0%	1	.1%
Food items	217	20.1%	589	54.4%	127	11.7%	79	7.3%	70	6.5%
Fruits and Vegetables	308	28.5%	539	49.8%	84	7.8%	105	9.7%	46	4.3%
Manufactured goods	131	12.1%	547	50.6%	326	30.1%	78	7.2%	0	0.0%
Packer and Movers	137	12.7%	433	40.0%	388	35.9%	74	6.8%	50	4.6%
Supply of water	139	12.8%	363	33.5%	402	37.2%	129	11.9%	49	4.5%

Views of female respondents

Table 5.17 explains the female respondent's perception for efficiency related to mobility of goods. Here, the table shows there is a small percentage of female respondents who agree that the mobility of goods in all categories is strongly efficient. The table shows that only 26.1%) of respondents has agreed that mobility of Fruits and vegetables is very efficient, (17.3%) think the same about water supply and (15.7%) about food items. However, there is a significant percentage of female respondents who agree that the mobility of goods is efficient. The data reveals that (54.4%) of respondents have stated that the mobility of food items is efficient, (61.4%) think the same about manufactured goods, followed by (53.6%) about packers and movers, (47.5%) about construction material and (43.6%) about food items. Many of the respondents have also expressed that the mobility of goods is average in the city. The data explains that (27.8%) think mobility of construction material is average, (27.3%) think the same about packers and movers, (25.4%) feel the same about food items and (25.3%) feel the same about manufactured goods. The data also reveals that (12%) of females said that the mobility of construction material is not efficient, (11.6%) think the same about water supply and (10.2%) feel the same about fruits and vegetables. When it comes to the question of extremely inefficient, (13.4%) female respondents have viewed mobility of food items as extremely inefficient and (8.7%) feel that the water supply is extremely inefficient.

Table 5.17: Female perceptions of efficiency in mobility of goods

N = 873	Female									
	Very efficient		Efficient		Average		Not efficient		Extremely inefficient	
	N	N%	N	N%	N	N%	N	N%	N	N%
Food items	137	15.7%	381	43.6%	222	25.4%	16	1.8%	117	13.4%
Fruits and Vegetables	228	26.1%	355	40.7%	163	18.7%	89	10.2%	38	4.4%
Manufactured goods	106	12.3%	528	61.4%	218	25.3%	6	.7%	2	.2%
Construction material	110	12.6%	415	47.5%	243	27.8%	105	12.0%	0	0.0%
Supply of water	151	17.3%	370	42.4%	175	20.0%	101	11.6%	76	8.7%
Packer and Movers	110	12.6%	468	53.6%	238	27.3%	12	1.4%	45	5.2%

5.13 Perceptions about the transport system for removal of waste material

Male perception

Table 5.18 shows the perceptions of male respondents about the transport system for removal of waste material. The waste materials here are classified into six categories:

- Agricultural waste
- Construction/demolition waste
- Electronic sources waste
- Industrial waste
- Medical/Clinical waste
- Municipal waste

The respondents were asked to give their opinion as very efficient, efficient, average, not efficient and extremely inefficient. The table shows that a majority of respondents agree with the option of efficient and average. (39.6%) of male respondents have viewed the mobility for medical/clinical waste as efficient, (32%) think transportation of industrial waste as efficient, (31.9%) think the same about removal of agricultural waste, (31.2%) about municipal waste and (30.5%) about electronic waste. The table shows (23.6%) of respondents have stated that the transport system is very efficient for the removal of medical/clinical waste, followed by (17.9%) who think the same about agricultural waste and a small percentage of respondents have agreed that the transport system for the removal of other waste materials is very efficient. For instance, (11%) agreed the same about industrial waste and (9.1%) about construction/demolition sources of waste.

When it comes to the question of average performance, the data shows that (39.6%) of respondents have marked removal of electronic waste as average, (45.7%) feel the same about construction/demolition waste, (30.7%) feel the same about industrial waste and (30.4%) feel the same about agricultural waste, followed by other categories. When it comes to the question of not efficient or extremely inefficient, (27.2%) of respondents have viewed the mobility of municipal waste as not efficient, (17.3%) think the same about construction/demolition waste and (16%) feel the same about industrial waste. There is small percentage of respondents who think that mobility of goods is extremely inefficient except in the case of industrial waste (10.4%).

Table 5.18: Male perceptions for transport system for removal of waste material

N = 1082	Male									
	Very efficient		Efficient		Average		Not efficient		Extremely inefficient	
	N	N%	N	N%	N	N%	N	N%	N	N%
Agricultural sources of waste	194	17.9%	345	31.9%	329	30.4%	142	13.1%	72	6.7%
Construction/ demolition sources of waste	98	9.1%	226	20.9%	495	45.7%	187	17.3%	76	7.0%
Electronic sources of waste	109	10.1%	330	30.5%	428	39.6%	163	15.1%	52	4.8%
Industrial sources of waste	119	11.0%	346	32.0%	332	30.7%	173	16.0%	112	10.4%
Medical/Clinical sources of waste	255	23.6%	428	39.6%	234	21.6%	135	12.5%	30	2.8%
Municipal sources of waste	192	17.7%	338	31.2%	233	21.5%	294	27.2%	25	2.3%

Female perceptions

Table 5.19 explains the female perceptions about transport systems for removal of waste material. Here, the data shows that (53.2%) of female respondents have viewed the removal of agricultural waste as efficient, followed by (39.6%) who think that it is efficient for removal of medical/clinical waste,

(32.9%) shared that it is efficient for removal of industrial waste, (37.8%) shared that it is efficient for removal of municipal waste and (37.8%) shared that it is efficient for removal of electronic waste. Here, the table shows (24.2%) of respondents have viewed that the transport system is very efficient for the removal of medical/clinical waste, (20.3%) said the same about industrial waste and (15.7%) feel the same about construction/demolition waste. A small percentage of female respondents have agreed that the transport system for the removal of other waste materials is very efficient. For instance, (4.6%) think that it is very efficient for electronic waste and (7.9%) feel the same about agricultural sources of waste.

When it comes to the question of average perceptions regarding the removal of waste material, the table shows that (42.8%) of respondents shared that removal of medical/clinical waste is average, (40%) shared the same for removal of electronic waste and (29.7%) shared the same for removal of agricultural waste and a small percentage feel the same about the other categories shown in the Table 5.19. When it comes to the question of not efficient or extremely inefficient, (19.8%) of female respondents have agreed that removal of construction/demolition waste is not efficient, followed by (18.2%) who feel the same about municipal waste and (18.1%) feel the same about industrial sources of waste. There is a small percentage of female respondents who have said that the mobility of goods is extremely inefficient except for the mobility of industrial sources of waste (12.4%).

Table 5.19: Female perceptions for transport system for removal of waste material

N = 873	Female									
	Very efficient		Efficient		Average		Not efficient		Extremely inefficient	
	N	N%	N	N%	N	N%	N	N%	N	N%
Agricultural sources of waste	69	7.9%	464	53.2%	259	29.7%	73	8.4%	8	.9%
Construction/ demolition sources of waste	137	15.7%	335	38.4%	162	18.6%	173	19.8%	66	7.6%
Electronic sources of waste	40	4.6%	330	37.8%	349	40.0%	89	10.2%	65	7.4%
Industrial sources of waste	177	20.3%	287	32.9%	143	16.4%	158	18.1%	108	12.4%
Medical/ Clinical sources of waste	211	24.2%	172	19.7%	374	42.8%	76	8.7%	40	4.6%
Municipal sources of waste	118	13.5%	330	37.8%	223	25.5%	159	18.2%	43	4.9%

5.14 Priorities that requires immediate attention and in a decade

Priorities that requires immediate attention

Table 5.20 explains the gender wise short-term city vision of respondents. The study has covered both male and female respondents from the four cities. The respondents from different educational institutions eagerly expressed their perceptions about smart cities. The table shows that the short-term vision has been classified into five categories mentioned below

- Clean and Green City
- Smart Infrastructure
- Houses, Employment and Education for all
- Smart Governance
- Health facilities for all

The ranking had been done on the priority basis of short-term vision of the concerned female and male respondents. It has been noted that there is a significant difference between the male and female preferences.

Table 5.20 indicates male respondents have given 1st rank to clean and green city while females have given 3rd rank. The government of India has now laid down new models for clean and green city development. Respondents have expressed that New Delhi is becoming polluted because of the heavy transport system, establishment industry[3] and absence of proper waste management services. The pollution in the city is creating an unhealthy atmosphere which needs to be cleaned through initiatives like *Swachh Bharat Abhiyan*, plantation and environment awareness programmes. When it comes to priority of smart infrastructure, male respondents have ranked 4th and female ranked it 5th. Similarly, males ranked 2nd and females ranked 1st to house, employment and education. The respondents viewed that there are thousands

---

3   Delhi has about 25 industrial clusters. Most of them are in close to proximity to residential areas. Delhi has approximately 13 thermal power plants within a radius of 300 km of Delhi which also contribute to the pollution significantly.

of homeless people scattered around the city. Respondents replied that the homeless people in Delhi during winter and rainy seasons go through severe health problems.

According to the latest economic survey of Delhi, unemployment has been increasing at an alarming rate since 2013 and 9.12 lakh people did not have jobs (Economic Survey of Delhi 2016 - 2017 n.d.). This number has risen to 12.2 lakh in 2015 (Delhi witnesses rapid increase in unemployment 2017). Respondents have also replied that migrants are facing severe employment problems and they are often unable to find viable solutions to such situations. The respondents also viewed that there are thousands of people doing menial jobs like rickshaw pulling, rag picking and setting up small shops to survive. The respondents also expressed that education is the key factor to survive in society and a major means of livelihood (Status of Education in Delhi 2017). Despite being a national capital, learning level among students in Delhi remains poor (Chettri 2017). The concerned authorities must prioritize the area of education.

In their interviews, many female respondents said that the increasing incidence of sexual harassment and violence against women in public spaces in cities has brought the issue of women's safety into the public discourse. Many have replied there is need of strong governance in the fields of policing, public bus service and night shelters for women and inadequacy of authorities to take pollution preventive measures throughout the years.

The data indicates that males ranked 3rd and females ranked 5th to healthy facilities for all. The respondents have viewed that Delhi's air pollution is causing a health crisis linked to allergies, respiratory conditions, birth malformations and increasing incidence of cancer. Delhi has limited government hospitals and health facilities for poor people. Thousands of patients are forced to wait on the hospital floors and do not even get adequate attention by the doctors. So, the current health infrastructure is not able to meet the needs of the increasing population.

Table 5.20: Priorities that requires immediate attention

Priorities	Male, N = 1082	Female, N = 873
Clean and Green City	2	1
Smart Infrastructure	4	2
Houses, Employment and Education for all	5	4
Smart Governance	1	3
Health facilities for all	3	5

Priorities that requires attention in a decade

Table 5.21 explains gender wise long-term city vision of respondents in all four cities taken into consideration. The table shows that long term vision has been divided into five categories such as:

- Clean and Green city
- Develop into world class city consisting of smart and efficient services
- Housing, employment, education for all
- Good medical facilities
- Smart and effective governance and citizen engagement

Table 5.21 explains that males ranked 5th and females ranked 3rd to clean and green city. Males ranked 4th and females ranked 1st to developing a word class city consisting of smart and efficient services. The data also shows males ranked 1st and females ranked 2nd to house, employment and education for all. Males ranked 1st and females ranked 5th to good medical facilities, males ranked 3rd and females ranked 4th to smart and effective governance and citizen engagement.

The data in the table shows that the long-term vision for both male and female respondents have big differences. Female respondent's priorities focus more on housing, education and employment. The respondents viewed that the increasing inward migration is a big issue and it is putting a pressure on living space. To accommodate the increasing population, housing and employment facilities should be a top priority for the government. Similarly, the male respondents have prioritized good medical facilities, smart and effective governance and citizen engagement. As per the view of respondent's, good medical facilities are required to meet the health issues of the increasing urban population. Citizen convenience through good governance will create a sustainable and healthy public platform and indulge the common citizen in various development activities.

Table 5.21: Priorities that requires attention in a decade

Priorities	Male, N = 1082	Female, N = 873
Clean and Green city	5	3
Develop into world class city consisting of smart and efficient services	4	1
House, employment, education for all	1	2
Good medical facilities	2	5
Smart and effective governance and citizen engagement	3	4

5.15 Current challenges faced by respondents

A healthy city life depends on the availability of facilities and infrastructure in the city itself. They have direct implications on development of our economy, society and environment. Table 5.22 analyses the gender wise challenges and current state of basic infrastructure in the city. The data shows that there are multiple challenges which need to be addressed adequately for the development of a smart city. The study indicates that according to male respondents, the major challenges are increasing traffic (92.9%), rise in pollution (91%), decline in greenery and cleanliness (83.6%), poverty (77.2%), increasing crime rate (70.6%), poor governance (68%), low job opportunities and quality (74.4%), water problem (68.5%) and sewage and sanitation problem (68.1%). At the same time, male respondents also said that there are no major challenges in the areas of energy efficiency (24★7 Electricity) (47.8%), Fall/drop in tourism (46.9%), Infrastructure issues (house, roads) (46.6%), lack of quality hospitals (37.0%) and increasing housing rate (35%).

Similarly, the data shows that the major current challenges faced by female respondents are increasing traffic (92.1%), increasing crime rate (88.1%) and rise in pollution (86.5%), sewage and sanitation problem (80.5%), poverty (77.2%) and decline in greenery & cleanliness (77.7%). The table below indicates that female respondents also said that there are no major challenges in the areas of energy efficiency (24★7 electricity) (58.3%), fall/drop in tourism (51.9%), lack of quality hospitals (41.4%) and water problems (43.6%). Based on the above analyses, it is evident that the major challenges faced by male respondents are increased traffic and rise in pollutions, while the major challenges for the female respondents are increased crime rate and sanitation problems.

Table 5.22: Current challenges faced by youth

N=1955	Male				Female			
	Yes		No		Yes		No	
	N	N%	N	N%	N	N%	N	N%
Decline in Greenery & Cleanliness	905	83.6%	177	16.4%	678	77.7%	195	22.3%
Drop in Cultural values	728	67.3%	354	32.7%	574	65.8%	299	34.2%
Energy efficiency (24*7 Electricity)	565	52.2%	517	47.8%	364	41.7%	509	58.3%
Fall/drop in tourism	575	53.1%	507	46.9%	420	48.1%	453	51.9%
Increased crime rates	764	70.6%	318	29.4%	769	88.1%	104	11.9%
Increased Traffic	1005	92.9%	77	7.1%	804	92.1%	69	7.9%
Increasing housing rates	703	65.0%	379	35.0%	624	71.5%	249	28.5%
Infrastructure issues (house, roads)	578	53.4%	504	46.6%	629	72.1%	244	27.9%
Job opportunities and quality	805	74.4%	277	25.6%	558	63.9%	315	36.1%
Lack of Quality of hospitals	682	63.0%	400	37.0%	512	58.6%	361	41.4%
Poor governance	653	60.4%	429	39.6%	681	78.0%	192	22.0%
Poverty	835	77.2%	247	22.8%	704	80.6%	169	19.4%
Rise in pollution	986	91.1%	96	8.9%	755	86.5%	118	13.5%
Sewerage/Sanitation issues	737	68.1%	345	31.9%	703	80.5%	170	19.5%
Water problems	741	68.5%	341	31.5%	492	56.4%	381	43.6%

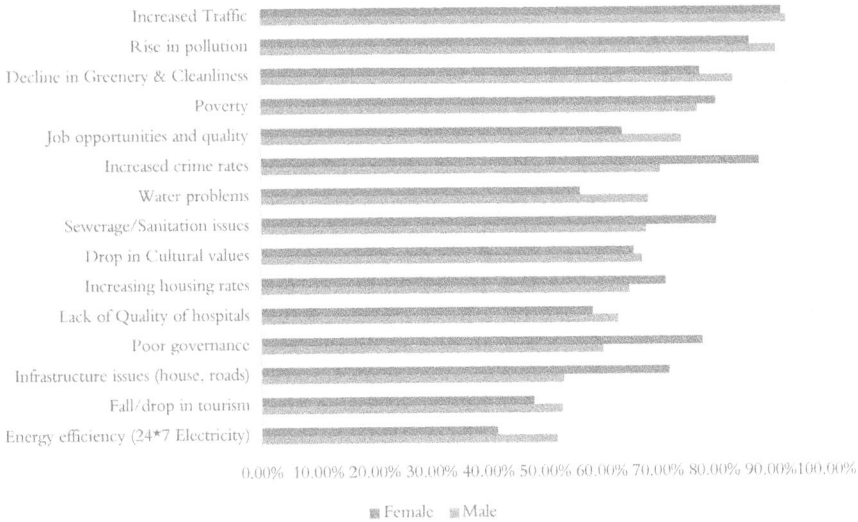

Figure 5.11: Current challenges faced by youth

5.16 Perceived Improvement of challenges in the next five years

Both male and female respondents also expressed their views on perceived improvement of challenges in the next five years. Table 5.23 shows that perceived improvement of challenges in the next five years. The data highlights that (46%) of male respondents feels that infrastructure related to roads and housing will improve, whereas (60%) of female respondents shared that infrastructure will improve in the next five years. Similarly, the table shows the other challenges as well which is perceived to decline or get worse in the next five years.

Table 5.23: Perceived improvement of challenges in the next five years

	Male, N = 1082			Female, N = 873		
	Will Improve	Will Decrease	Will get worse	Will Improve	Will Decrease	Will get worse
Crime rates	44%	38%	18%	30%	54%	15%
Energy efficiency (24*7 Electricity)	76%	17%	7%	79%	11%	11%
Greenery & Cleanliness	77%	16%	7%	84%	15%	1%
Housing rates	47%	32%	21%	46%	33%	21%
Infrastructure issues (house, roads)	46%	52%	3%	60%	38%	1%
Job opportunities and quality	41%	42%	17%	39%	50%	11%
Pollution Level	53%	29%	17%	45%	34%	21%
Poor governance	54%	33%	14%	46%	37%	17%
Poverty	73%	18%	9%	71%	27%	2%
Quality of hospitals	52%	37%	10%	66%	27%	7%
Sewerage/Sanitation issues	55%	38%	7%	58%	30%	12%
Tourism Footfall	54%	43%	3%	53%	45%	2%
Traffic	56%	39%	5%	49%	43%	8%
Water Availability	43%	31%	26%	39%	37%	24%

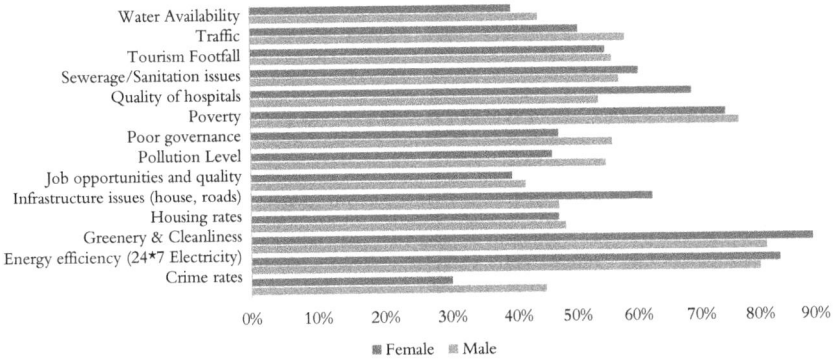

Figure 5.12: Perceived improvement of challenges in the next five years

5.17 Prioritization of features in making the surveyed city as a smart city

Table 5.24 shows the gender wise views on prioritization of features in making their city into a smart city. According to male respondents, high priority areas are air quality, economy and employment, education, energy efficiency, energy supply, health, safety and security, sanitation, waste water management and water supply and their frequencies are more than (80%). For female respondents, high priority areas are education, economy and employment, health, safety and security, waste water management and water supply and their frequencies are more than (80%). There are other areas as well which are highly prioritized and non-prioritized as shown in the table below.

Table 5.24: Prioritization of features in making surveyed as a smart city

N=1955	Male				Female			
	High Priority	Medium Priority	Low Priority	Not at all Important	High Priority	Medium Priority	Low Priority	Not at all Important
Air Quality	85%	14%	0%	0%	78%	22%	0%	0%
Citizen Engagement	62%	31%	7%	0%	51%	35%	11%	2%
City Identity and Culture	69%	22%	10%	0%	52%	43%	0%	4%
Compact City	73%	8%	19%	0%	35%	45%	17%	3%
Economy and Employment	87%	5%	8%	0%	79%	18%	3%	0%
Education	97%	2%	1%	0%	86%	14%	0%	0%
Energy Efficiency	80%	15%	5%	0%	65%	26%	9%	0%
Energy Supply	87%	11%	2%	0%	79%	18%	3%	0%
Health	94%	5%	1%	0%	82%	17%	3%	0%
Housing and Inclusiveness	69%	26%	4%	1%	50%	49%	1%	0%

N=1955	Male				Female			
	High Priority	Medium Priority	Low Priority	Not at all Important	High Priority	Medium Priority	Low Priority	Not at all Important
Intelligent Govt. Services	79%	12%	9%	0%	71%	26%	2%	2%
IT connectivity	77%	5%	18%	0%	56%	34%	9%	0%
Public Open Spaces	68%	14%	17%	1%	34%	47%	17%	0%
Safety and Security	95%	3%	1%	0%	85%	15%	0%	0%
Sanitation	89%	10%	2%	0%	68%	25%	7%	0%
Transportation	78%	19%	1%	1%	58%	41%	0%	0%
Underground Electric Wiring	77%	17%	5%	1%	56%	41%	3%	0%
Walkable	82%	13%	5%	0%	47%	42%	11%	0%
Waste Water management	96%	4%	0%	0%	77%	22%	0%	0%
Water Management	90%	9%	1%	0%	80%	18%	2%	0%
Water Supply	92%	7%	1%	0%	83%	17%	0%	0%

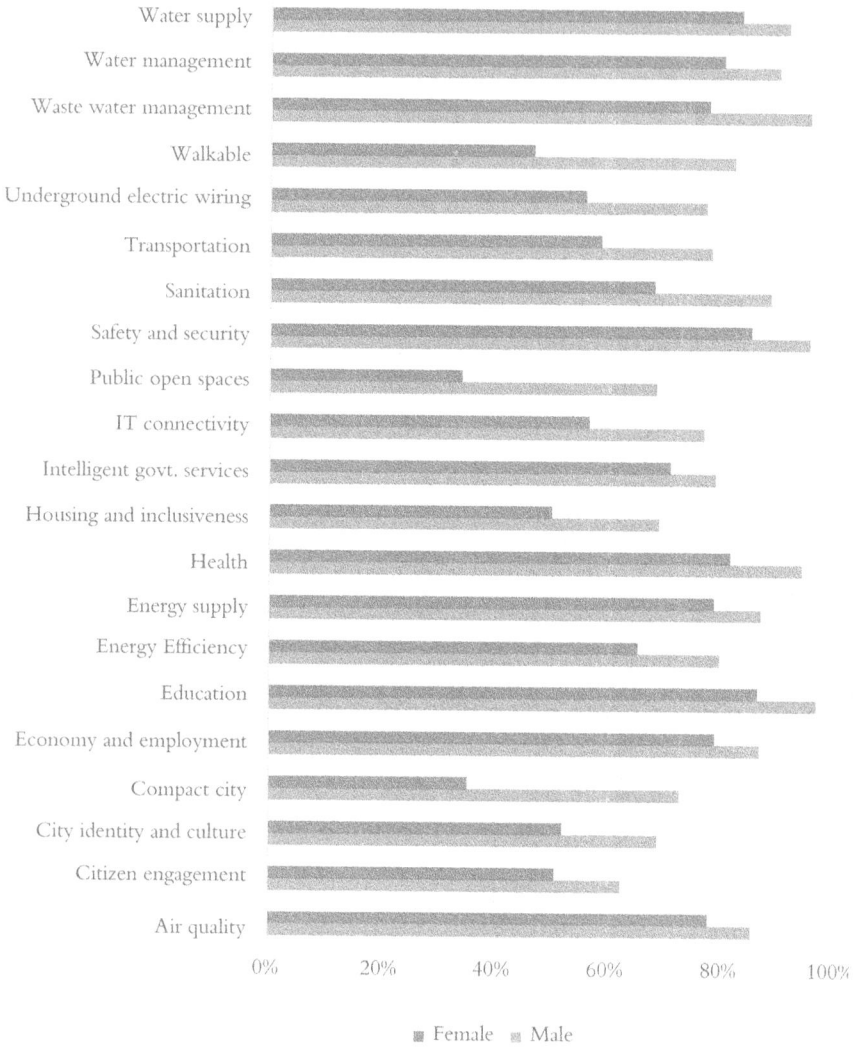

Figure 5.13: Prioritization of features in making surveyed as a smart city

Chapter 6
Perceptions based on Income Group

This chapter highlights the income group perceptions of respondents on mobility related areas such as commuting time, money involved in commuting, consumers satisfaction level, existing problems with public transport system and their safety, their perceptions for the services which are likely to improve in the near future and their expectations from Government & policy makers to encourage green transport in the cities. It also highlights the policy measures that should be initiated/strengthened to improve the urban transport system.

Perceptions related to green transport were also recorded to know the current efforts made by respondents. Questions related to mobility of goods and transport system of removal of waste material were also recorded. Respondents also shared their views about priorities that require immediate attention and in a decade for their cities. This chapter also highlights the current challenges faced by respondents in their cities and perceived improvement approaches for the next five years.

6.1 Factors related to Mobility

Respondents shared information regarding the time taken to commute to work or university. The data revealed that there is significant difference in the travel of up to two hours among all the income groups except those who travel more than two hours in a day.

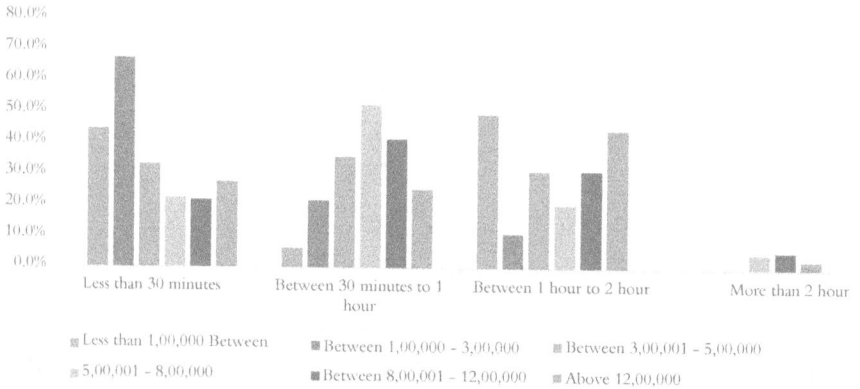

Figure 6.1: Time to commute from home to destination (income group in ₹)

Monthly expenditure

Two-third of respondents who are in the income group of ₹1 lakh to ₹3 lakh shared that their cost of mobility is between ₹1001– ₹3000 while using public transport. Half of the respondents from the same income group shared that the cost of mobility for them is between ₹1001– ₹3000. There was not a significant number of respondents (less than 20%) from all income groups who said that the cost of mobility is above ₹5000.

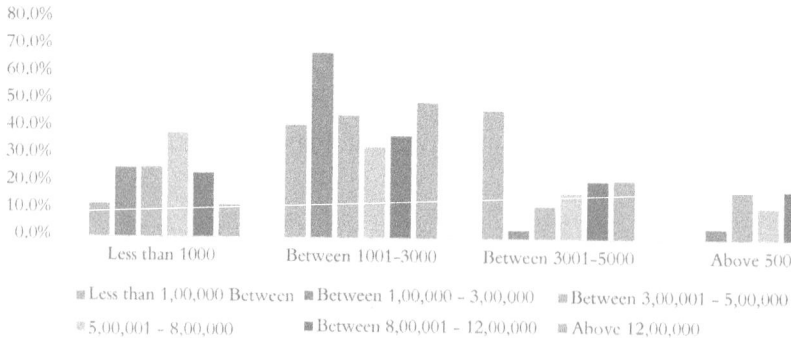

Figure 6.2: Monthly expenditure on mobility (income group in ₹)

Cost of mobility in next few years

More than (90%) of respondents from all income groups either strongly agree or agree that the cost of mobility is going to increase in the coming few years.

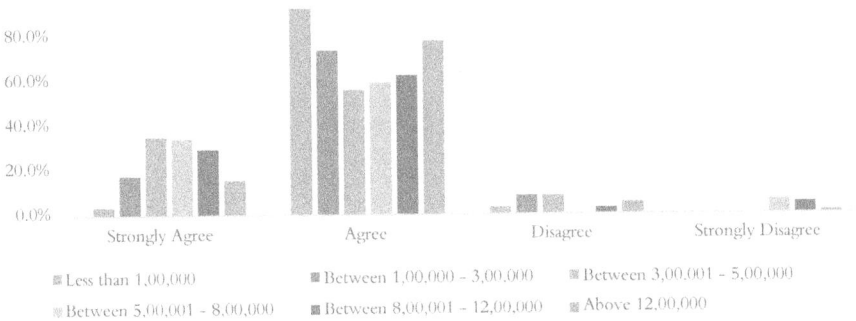

Figure 6.3: Cost of mobility in near future will increase over time (income group in ₹)

Level of satisfaction

The data from all income groups shows that respondents are somewhat satisfied with the time and money they spent on transport related facilities. In terms of respondents from the middle class (between ₹5 lakh and ₹8 lakh), more than (43%) are dissatisfied with the time and money spent on the transport mode.

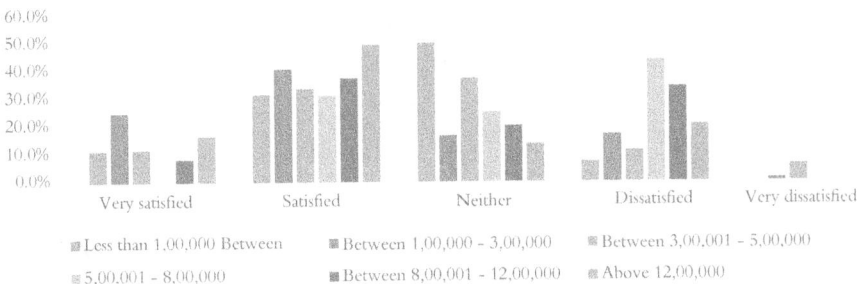

Figure 6.4: Satisfied with the time and money spend (income group in ₹)

6.2 Problems with public transport

All respondents from all income groups shared that the waiting period is too long for the preferred route in public transport. The data also highlights that more than (95%) of respondents from all income groups found that the public transport mode is not reliable especially during non-peak hours. For high income groups, availability of last mile connectivity is also a big issue. For all the income groups, over-crowded public transport is an issue.

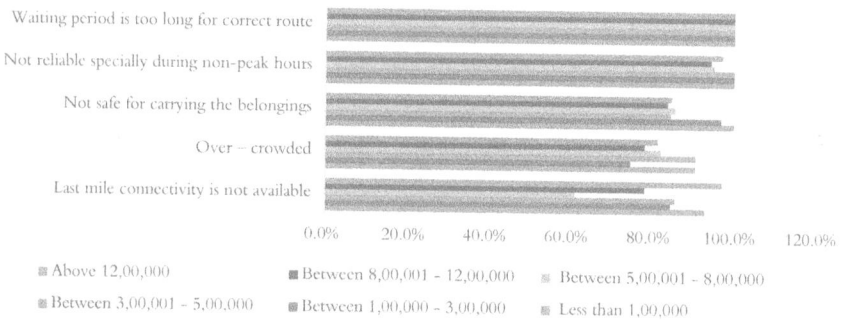

Figure 6.5: Problems with public transport (income group in ₹)

6.3 Personal safety in Public Transport

Data revealed that not even a single respondent from all income groups feels safe using public transport. More than (40%) of respondents find the personal safety average in public transport. This is alarming and limiting the number of daily commuters who use public transport.

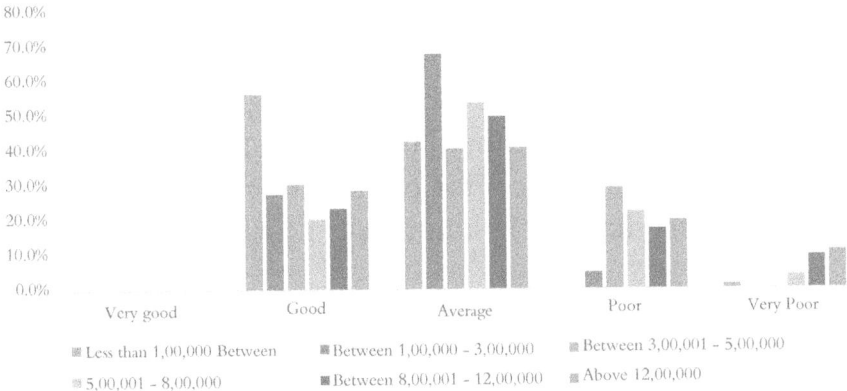

Figure 6.6: Personal safety in public transport (income group in ₹)

6.4 Services that may improve in next five years

The data highlights the views of respondents on the services that may improve in the next five years. There are several issues categorically mentioned here and each issue has its own significance for providing better transport system to the respondents. Respondents shared that parking management, traffic management and management of means of transport is going to be improved in next five years.

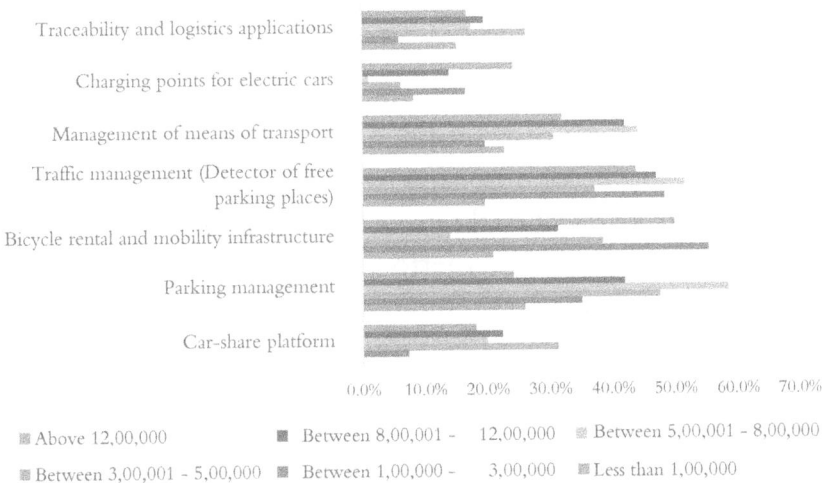

Figure 6.7: Services that may improve in next five years (income group in ₹)

6.5 Services may improve in near future

Respondents from all income groups shared that public transport and shared transport services are likely to be increased in the near future. The percentage of respondents who said that the services for private transport are going to improve is less than (20%) among all the age groups.

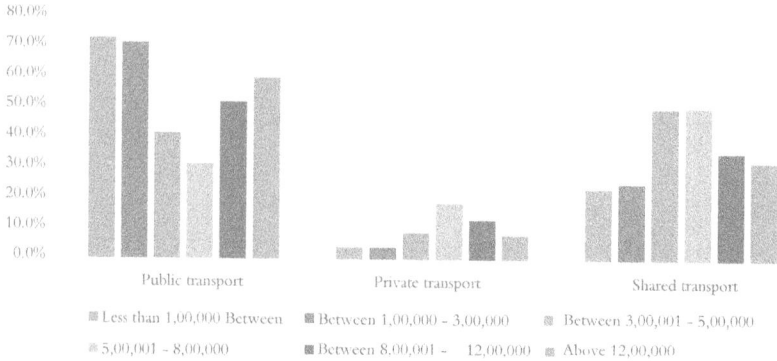

Figure 6.8: Services which may improve in near future (income group in ₹)

6.6 Transport mode that may improve in next five years

When it come to the question of what is expected to be better for public transport, the study shows metro is the best option for majority of respondents from all income groups. More than (60%) of respondents whose yearly income is between ₹5 lakh – ₹12 lakh and above ₹12 lakh shared that transport mode trains like metro will increase in the next five years.

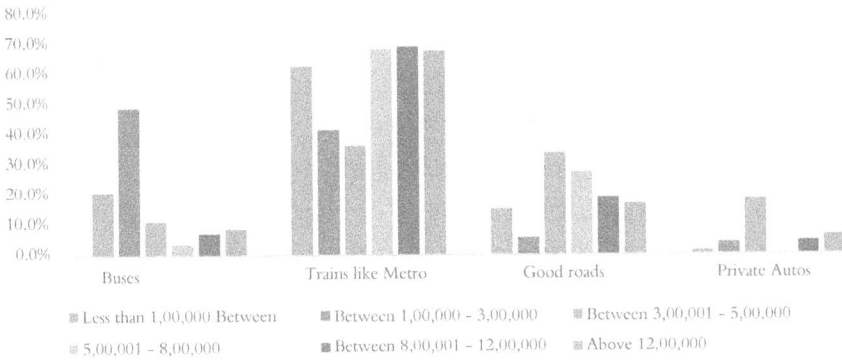

Figure 6.9: Transport mode that may improve in next five years (income group in ₹)

6.7 Willing to pay additional money for better transport

Figure 6.10 shows the willingness of people to pay additional money for better transportation. The data revealed that the percentage of respondents who are willing to pay more than ₹5000 is actually less than (12%) irrespective of their income levels.

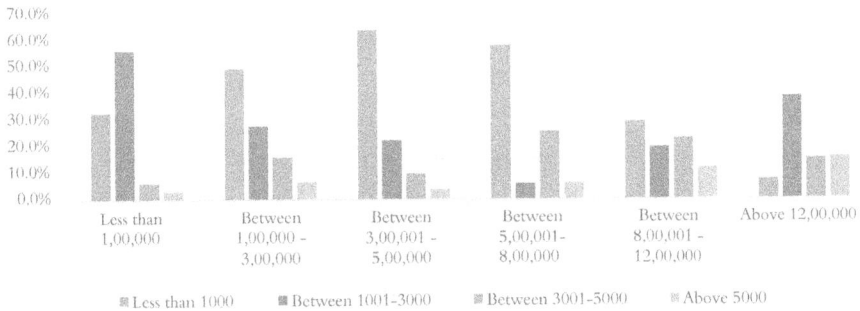

Figure 6.10: Willing to pay additional money for better transport (income group in ₹)

6.8 Suggested measures to promote green transport

The data revealed that more than (50%) of respondents from all income groups have given higher priority to building road networks to support green transport, infrastructural support by installing charging stations and ensuring sufficient supply of electricity for each family. The data also revealed that subsidies to manufacturers are also not significantly endorsed by the respondents.

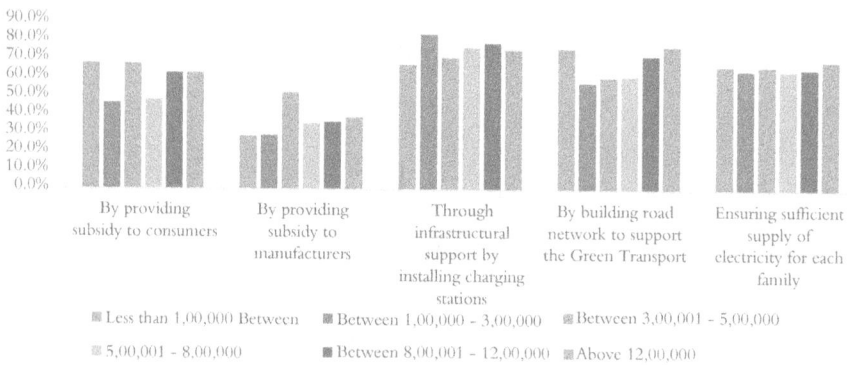

Figure 6.11: Suggested measures to promote green transport (income group in ₹)

6.9 Measures for improvement in urban transport system

More than (60%) of respondents from all income groups shared that the measure to improve the urban transport system can be done through restraining the use of polluting vehicles and fuels. More than (50%) of respondents from all income groups shared that the urban transport system can be made compliant for vehicle emission standards and inspection & maintenance and through encouraging green modes/transports.

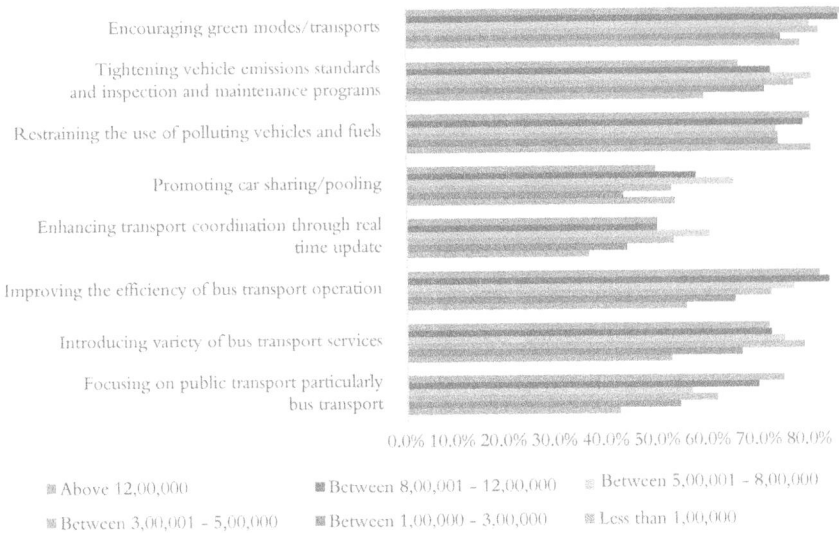

Figure 6.12: *Measures for improvement in urban transport system (income group in ₹)*

6.10 Perceptions for green transport

The responses from all income groups who agree with various statements is recorded in figure 6.13. Close to (70%) of respondents from income group of less than ₹1 lakh agreed with the statement that more than half of the vehicles in India will be replaced by electric vehicles in 20 years. (60%) from the same income group feel that there will be a fall in green transport prices in the near future. The same income group highlights the need of a network of charging facilities and considers it as a prerequisite for the use of green transport. They also feel that an automobile is a necessity for them and represents status in society, such a percentage is more than (60%) in the income group of less than ₹1 lakh.

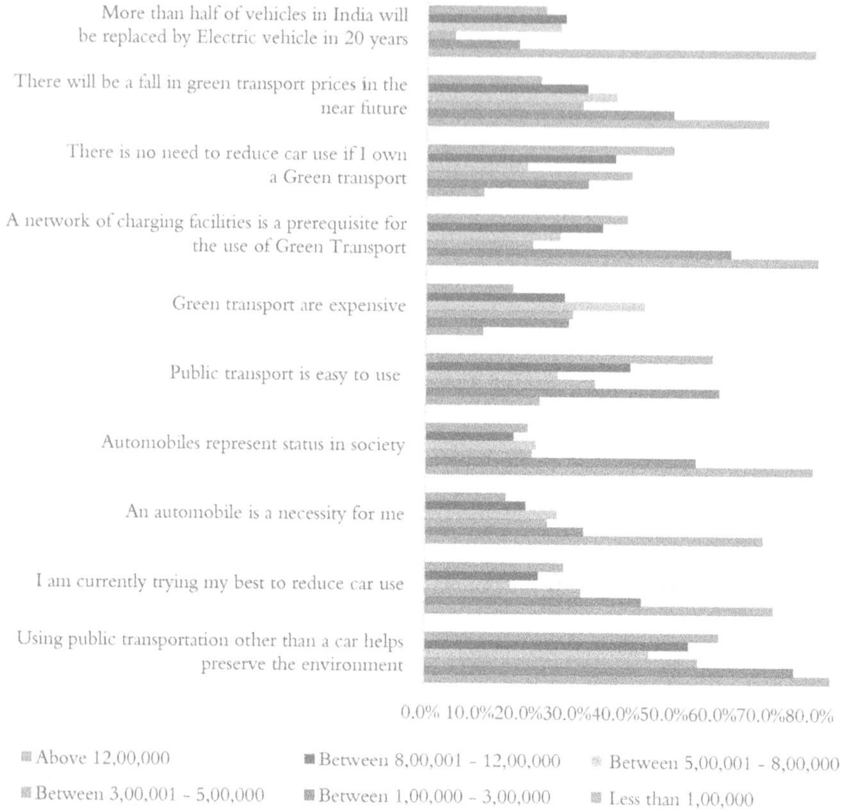
More than half of vehicles in India will be replaced by Electric vehicle in 20 years
There will be a fall in green transport prices in the near future
There is no need to reduce car use if I own a Green transport
A network of charging facilities is a prerequisite for the use of Green Transport
Green transport are expensive
Public transport is easy to use
Automobiles represent status in society
An automobile is a necessity for me
I am currently trying my best to reduce car use
Using public transportation other than a car helps preserve the environment
0.0% 10.0% 20.0% 30.0% 40.0% 50.0% 60.0% 70.0% 80.0%
Above 12,00,000
Between 8,00,001 - 12,00,000
Between 5,00,001 - 8,00,000
Between 3,00,001 - 5,00,000
Between 1,00,000 - 3,00,000
Less than 1,00,000

Figure 6.13: Perceptions for green transport (income group in ₹)

6.11 Perceptions of efficiency in mobility of goods

A significant percentage of respondents (greater than 50%) in the income group of ₹5 lakh to above ₹12 lakh consider the transport system of food items as efficient. A significant number of respondents shared that the efficiency related to mobility of goods such as packers and movers, water supply, fruits and vegetables, manufactured goods is efficient but there are still some requirements to make them more efficient.

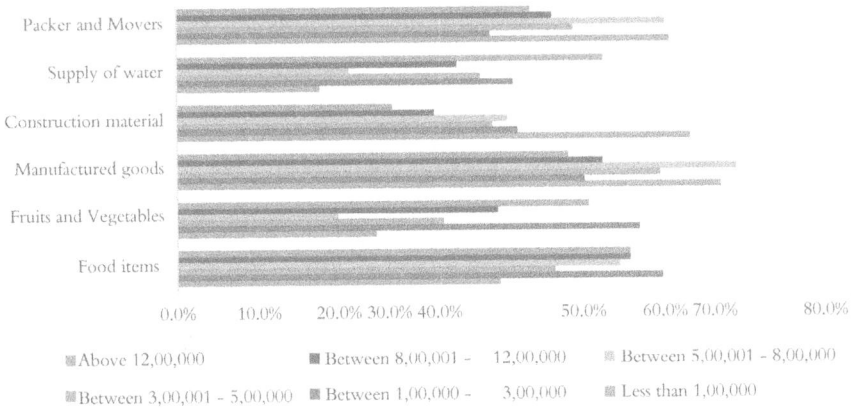

Figure 6.14: Perceptions of efficiency in mobility of goods (income group in ₹)

6.12 Perceptions about the transport system for removal of waste material

The data highlights the perceptions about the transport system for removal of waste material which is not efficient in Delhi-NCR and Lucknow. More than (50%) of respondents from the income group of less than ₹1 lakh shared that the transport system for removal of waste material such as construction/demolition waste, industrial waste and municipal waste is not efficient in the city. There are respondents, close to (45%) from the income group of ₹5 lakh to ₹8 lakh, who feel that the transport system for removal of waste for medical/clinical sources and municipal sources are not efficient. The respondents from income group of ₹1 lakh – ₹3 lakh shared that the waste removal mechanism for construction/demolition source is efficient.

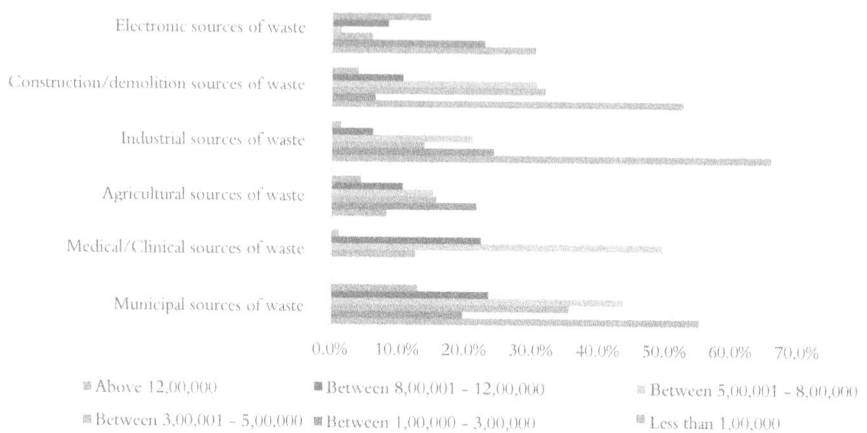

Figure 6.15: Perceptions for transport system for removal of waste material (Not Efficient) (income group in ₹)

6.13 Current challenges faced by youth

Figure 6.16 shows the current challenges faced by respondents in their respective cities. The data revealed that more than (50%) of respondents are facing challenges in infrastructure related issues[1], sewerage/sanitation related issues, job opportunities and job quality, increased crime rates, poor governance, increased poverty, lack of quality of hospitals, sudden rise in pollution and increased traffic. This shows that the respondents are facing many more issues in their life. Traffic congestion and modes of transport is one of the issues.

---

1 *Infrastructure related issues include road, streets and housing colonies.*

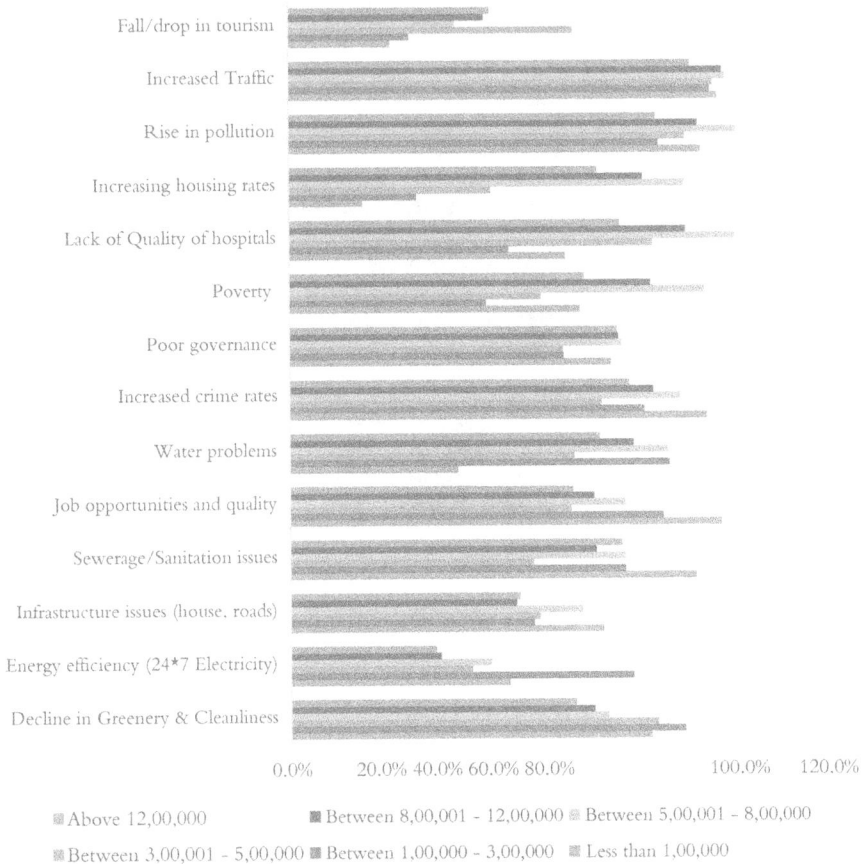

Fall/drop in tourism
Increased Traffic
Rise in pollution
Increasing housing rates
Lack of Quality of hospitals
Poverty
Poor governance
Increased crime rates
Water problems
Job opportunities and quality
Sewerage/Sanitation issues
Infrastructure issues (house, roads)
Energy efficiency (24*7 Electricity)
Decline in Greenery & Cleanliness

0.0%   20.0% 40.0% 60.0% 80.0%   100.0%   120.0%

▣ Above 12,00,000   ▣ Between 8,00,001 - 12,00,000 ▣ Between 5,00,001 – 8,00,000
▣ Between 3,00,001 - 5,00,000 ▣ Between 1,00,000 – 3,00,000   ▣ Less than 1,00,000

Figure 6.16: Current challenges faced by youth (income group in ₹)

6.14 Perceived Improvement of challenges in the next five years

The respondents have expressed their views on perceived improvements of challenges in the next five years. The major challenges in the income group of less than ₹3 lakh are quality of hospitals, poverty, water availability, job opportunities and job quality, infrastructure (houses and roads) and availability of electricity.

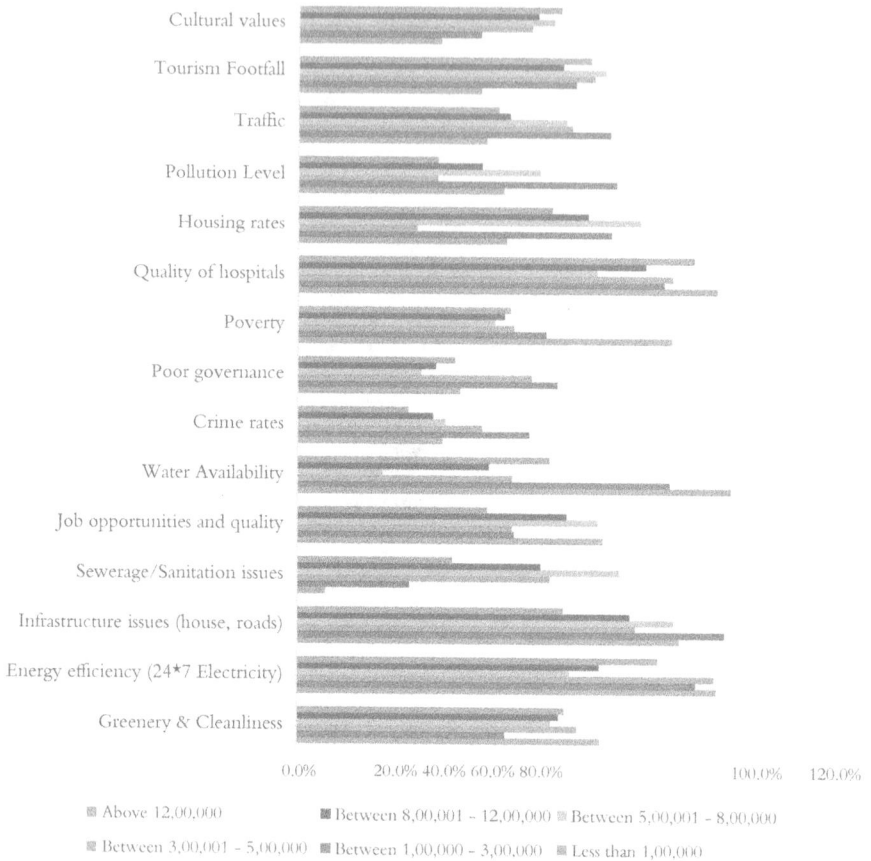

Figure 6.17: Perceived Improvement of challenges in the next five years (income group in ₹)

6.15 Prioritization of interventions

The respondents have expressed their views about prioritization of features in making their city into a smart city. The data revealed that education, health, water management, air quality, water management, economy and employment are more important in all income groups.

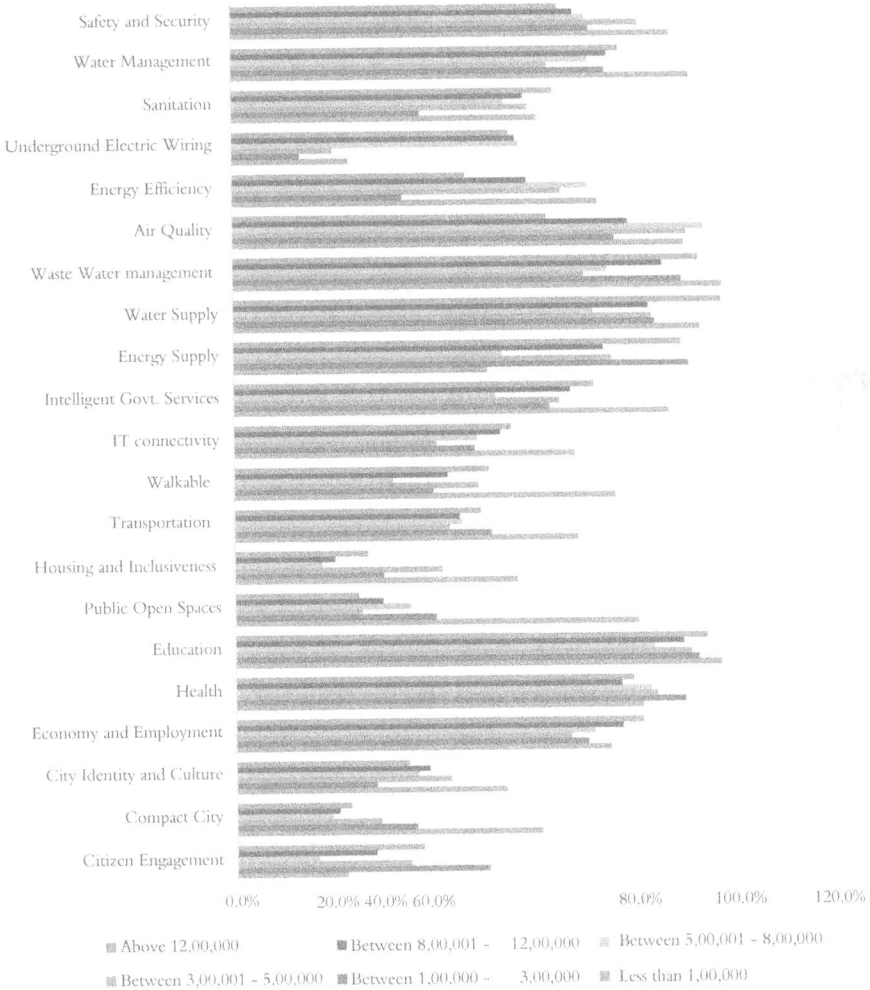

Figure 6.18: Prioritization of interventions (income group in ₹)

Chapter 7
Perceptions based on education

This chapter highlights the educational perceptions of respondents on mobility related issues such as commuting time, money involved in commuting, consumer satisfaction, existing problems with public transport system and their personal safety, their perceptions for the services which are likely to improve in the near future and their expectations from Government and policy makers to encourage green transport in the cities. It also highlights the policy measures that should be initiated/strengthened to improve the urban transport system.

Perceptions related to automobile and green transport were also recorded to know the current efforts made by respondents. Questions related to mobility of goods and transport system of removal of waste material were also recorded. Respondents also shared their views about short-term and long-term visions for their cities. This chapter also highlights the current challenges faced by respondents in their current cities and perceived improvement approaches for the next five years.

Education Level and Income Group

During the data analysis, it was found that there is a statically significant correlation between the education level and income group.

Table 7.1: Education level and income group

	Income Level (in ₹)					
Education Group	Less than 1,00,000	Between 1,00,000 – 3,00,000	Between 3,00,001 – 5,00,000	Between 5,00,001 – 8,00,000	Between 8,00,001 – 12,00,000	Above 12,00,000
Under Graduate	134	278	434	220	138	320
Graduate	12	45	53	40	19	65
Post Graduate	10	30	58	29	21	49
Total	**156**	**353**	**545**	**289**	**178**	**434**

7.1 Factors related to mobility

Respondents shared information regarding time taken to commute to destination. The data revealed that there is no significant difference in the travel pattern up to two hours among all education groups.

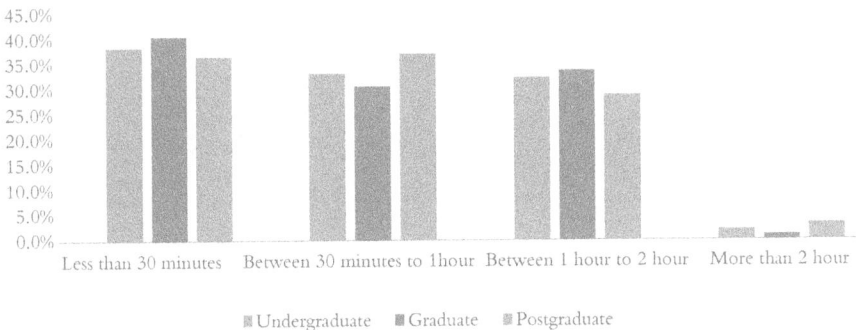

Figure 7.1: Time to commute from home to destination (One side travel)

Monthly expenditure

Responses were recorded for monthly expenditure by the respondents. It was observed that there is no significant difference in expenditure pattern.

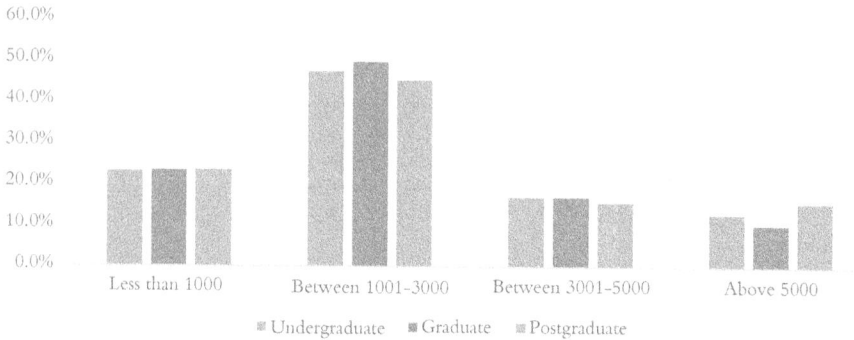

Undergraduate *Graduate* *Postgraduate*

Figure 7.2: Monthly expenditure on mobility (in ₹)

Cost of mobility in next few years

More than (90%) of respondents from all education groups either strongly agree or agree that the cost of mobility is going to increase in the coming few years.

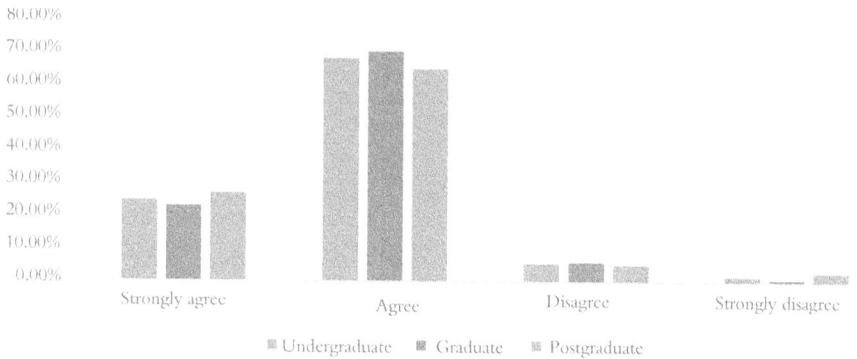

Undergraduate *Graduate* *Postgraduate*

Figure 7.3: Cost of mobility in near future will increase over time

Level of satisfaction

Respondents from all education groups are satisfied up to a large extent with the time and money spent by them on transport related facilities. However, there is a significant percentage (around 20% or less) in all education groups who are dissatisfied with the time and money spent by them on transport related facilities.

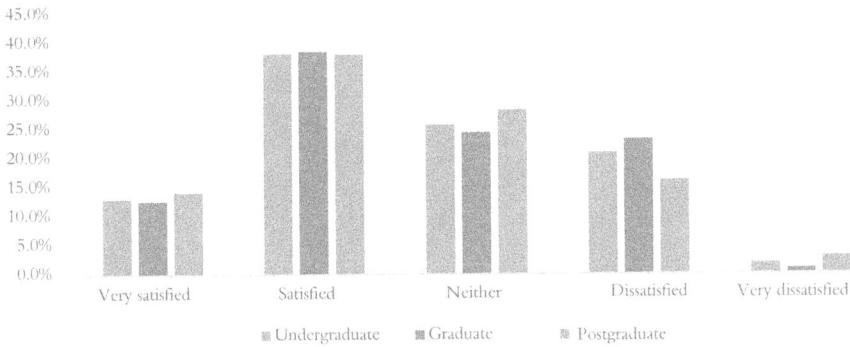

Figure 7.4: Satisfied with this time and money spend

7.2 Problems with Public Transport

All respondents from all education groups shared that the waiting period is too long for preferred route in public transport. The data highlights that more than (80%) of respondents from all education groups found public transport modes as unreliable especially during non-peak hours.

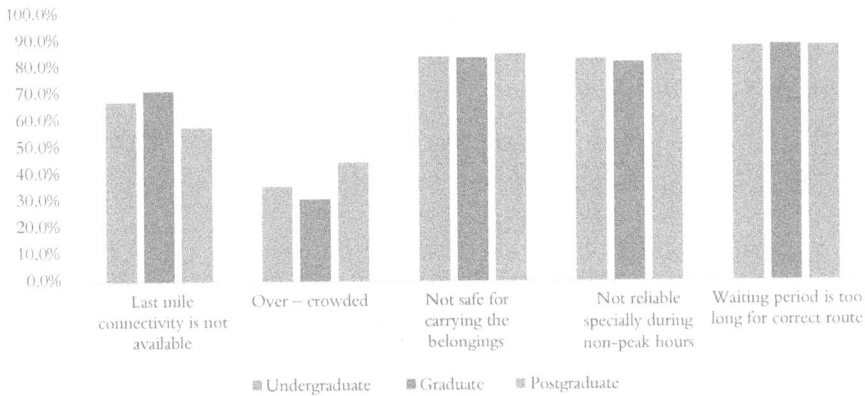

Figure 7.5: Problems with public transport

7.3 Personal safety in Public Transport

The data revealed that not even a single respondent from any of the education groups feels safe in public transport. More than (40%) of respondents find personal safety average in public transport. This is alarming and limiting the daily commuters who use public transport.

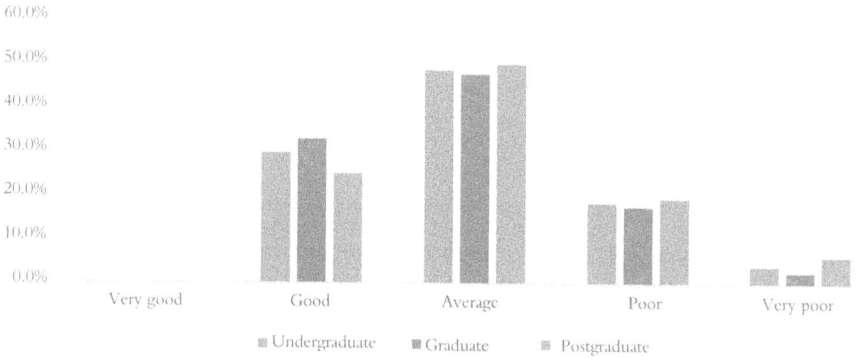

Figure 7.6: Personal safety in public transport

7.4 Services that may improve in next five years

The data highlights the views of respondents on services that will improve in the next five years. There are several issues categorically mentioned here and each issue has its own significance for providing better transport system to the respondents. Respondents shared that parking management, traffic management and management of means of transport is going to improve in next five years.

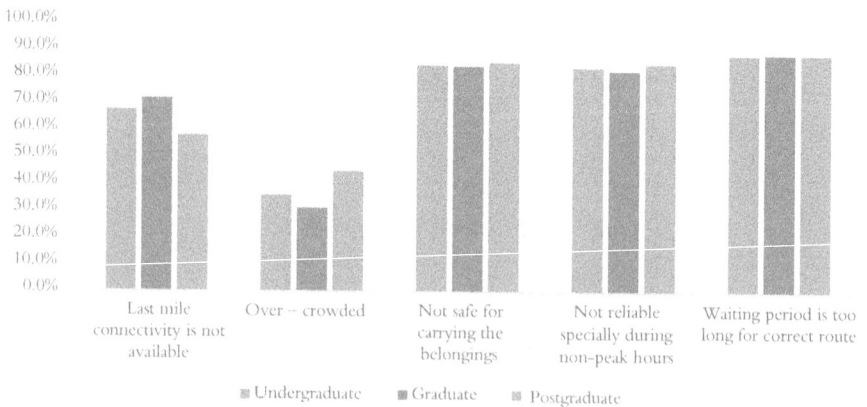

Figure 7.7: Services that may improve in next five years

7.5 Perception about services that are likely to be improved in the near future

Respondents from all age groups shared that the public transport and shared transport services are likely to increase in the near future. The percentage of respondents who shared that the services for private transport are going to improve is less than (20%) among all age groups.

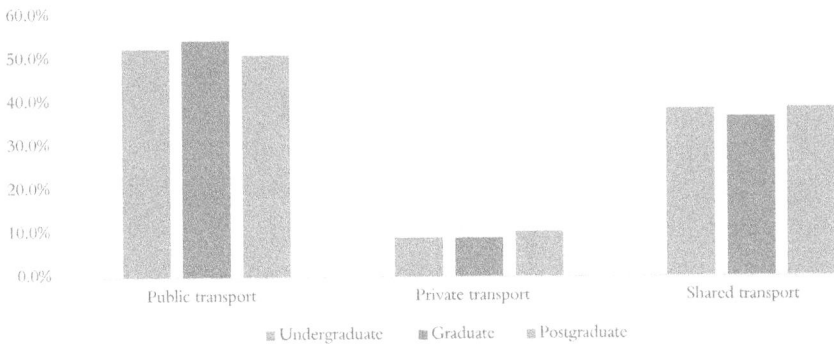

Figure 7.8: Perception on services that are likely to be improved in near future

7.6 Transport mode that may improve in next five years

When it comes to the question of what is expected to be better for public transport, the study shows that the metro is the best option for majority of respondents from all education groups. More than (50%) of respondents from all education groups shared that in terms of transport modes, trains like metro are going to increase in the next five years.

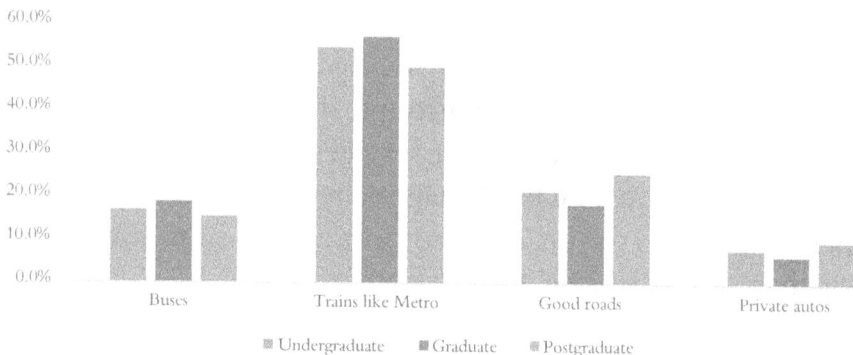

Figure 7.9: Transport mode that may improve in next five years

7.7 Willing to pay additional money for better transport

Figure 7.10 shows the willingness of people to pay additional money for better transportation. The data revealed that the percentage of respondents who are willing to pay more than ₹5000 is actually less than (10%) irrespective of their education levels.

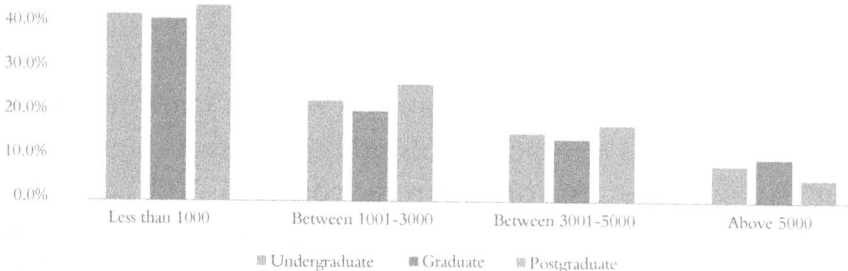

Figure 7.10: Willing to pay additional money for better transport (Amount in ₹)

7.8 Suggested measures to promote green transport

Figure 7.11 shows that more than (60%) of respondents from all education groups have given more priority to building road networks to support green transport, infrastructural support by installing charging stations and ensuring sufficient supply of electricity for each family.

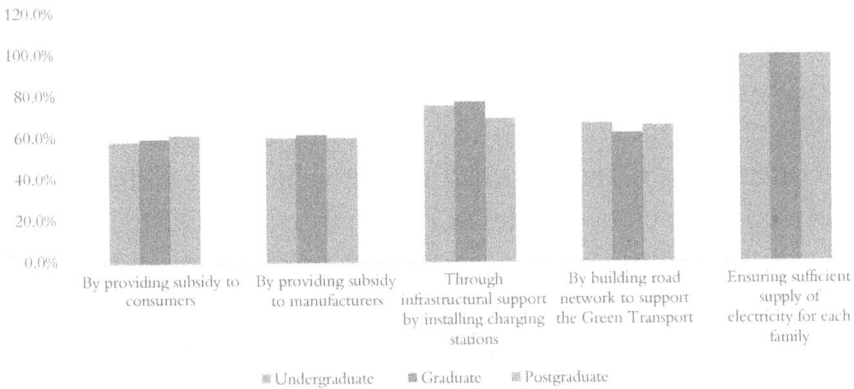

Figure 7.11: Suggested measures to promote green transport

7.9 Measures for improvement in urban transport system

More than (60%) of respondents from all education groups shared that one of the measures to improve the urban transport system is restraining the use of polluting vehicles and fuels. More than (50%) of respondents from all education group shared that the urban transport system can be made more efficient by ensuring compliance for vehicle emission standards and inspection & maintenance and through encouraging green modes/transports.

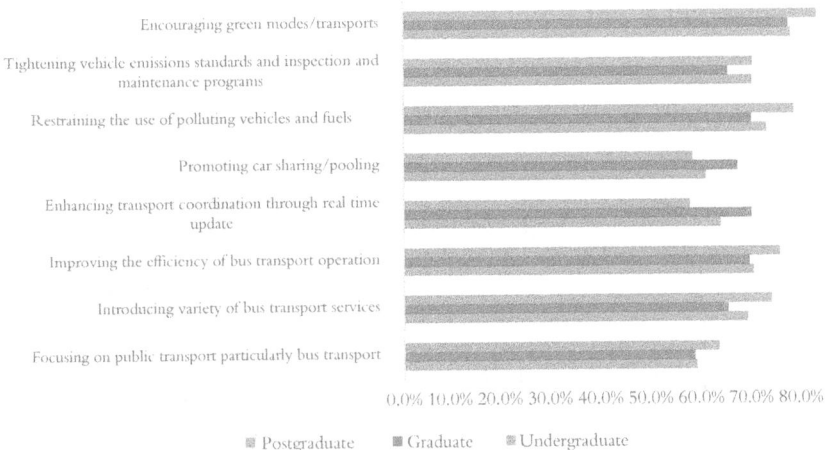

Figure 7.12: Measures for improvement in urban transport system

7.10 Perceptions about green transport

The responses from all education groups who agree with various statements is recorded in the Figure 7.13. Close to (35%) of respondents from all education group agreed with the statement that more than half of the vehicles in India will be replaced by electric vehicles in 20 years. Less than (20%) from all education groups feel that there will be a fall in green transport prices in the near future. Only less than (10%) of students from all education groups believe that green transport is expensive. It can be concluded that education does not play a significant role in creating differences in perceptions amongst youth.

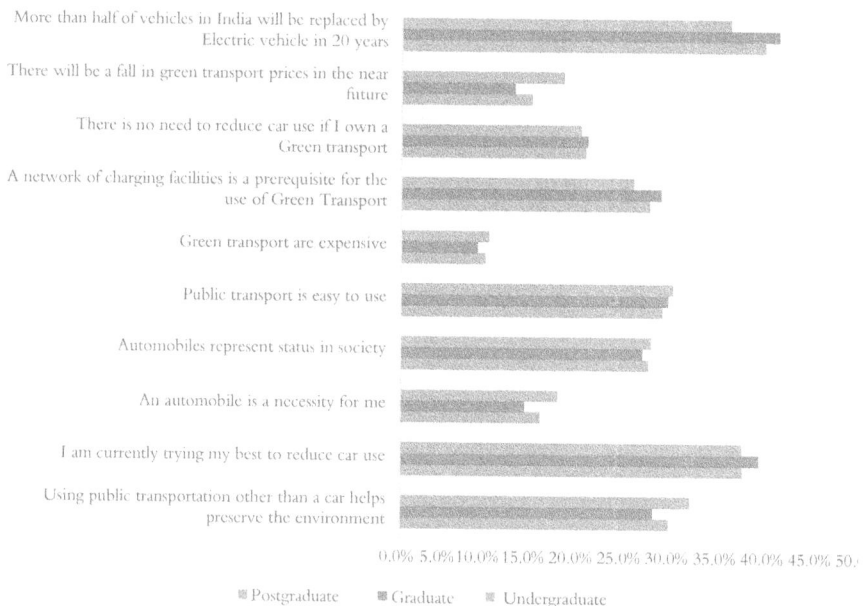

Figure 7.13: Perceptions for green transport

7.11 Perceptions of efficiency in mobility of goods

Respondents were asked about their perceptions regarding efficiency related to mobility of goods. It was observed that the perception of respondents who had completed their graduation degree is marginally higher than other education groups.

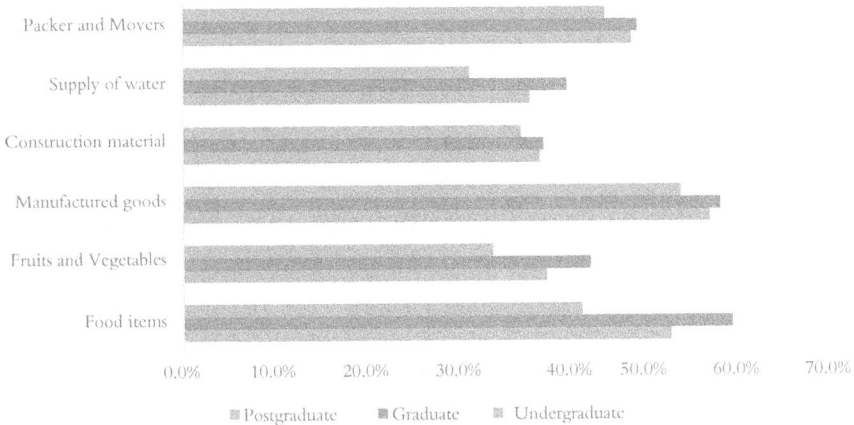

Figure 7.14: Perceptions of efficiency in mobility of goods

7.12 Perceptions for transport system for removal of waste material

The data highlights perceptions about the transport system for removal of agricultural waste which is not efficient in Delhi-NCR and Lucknow. More than (20%) of respondents from all education group shared the transport system for removal of waste material such as construction/demolition waste, industrial waste and municipal waste is not efficient in the city.

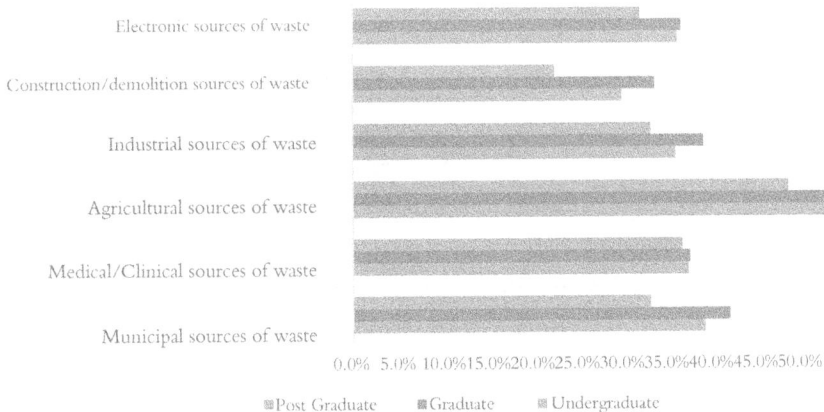

Figure 7.15: Perceptions for transport system for removal of waste material

7.13 Current challenges faced by youth

Figure 7.16 shows the current challenges faced by respondents in their respective cities. The data revealed that more than (40%) of the respondents are facing challenges in infrastructure related issues, sewerage/sanitation related issues, job opportunities and their quality, increased crime rates, poor governance, increased poverty, lack of quality of hospitals, sudden rise in pollution and increased traffic.

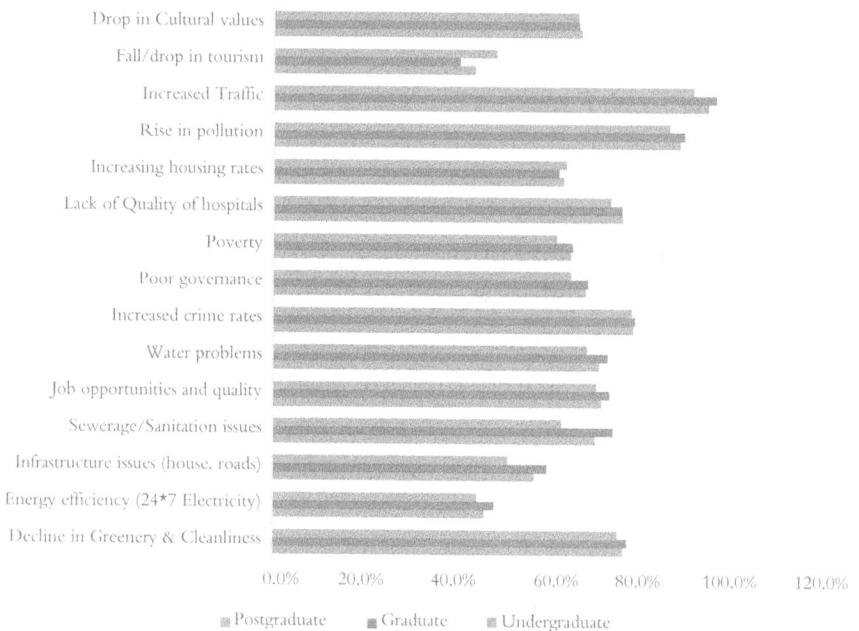

Figure 7.16: Current challenges faced by youth

7.14 Perceived improvement of challenges in the next five years

The respondents have expressed their views about perceived improvement of challenges in the next five years. There is no significant difference in the perceptions of all education groups. The major challenges which might be improved in the next five years are quality of hospitals, infrastructure related to roads and houses, energy efficiency, greenery and cleanliness.

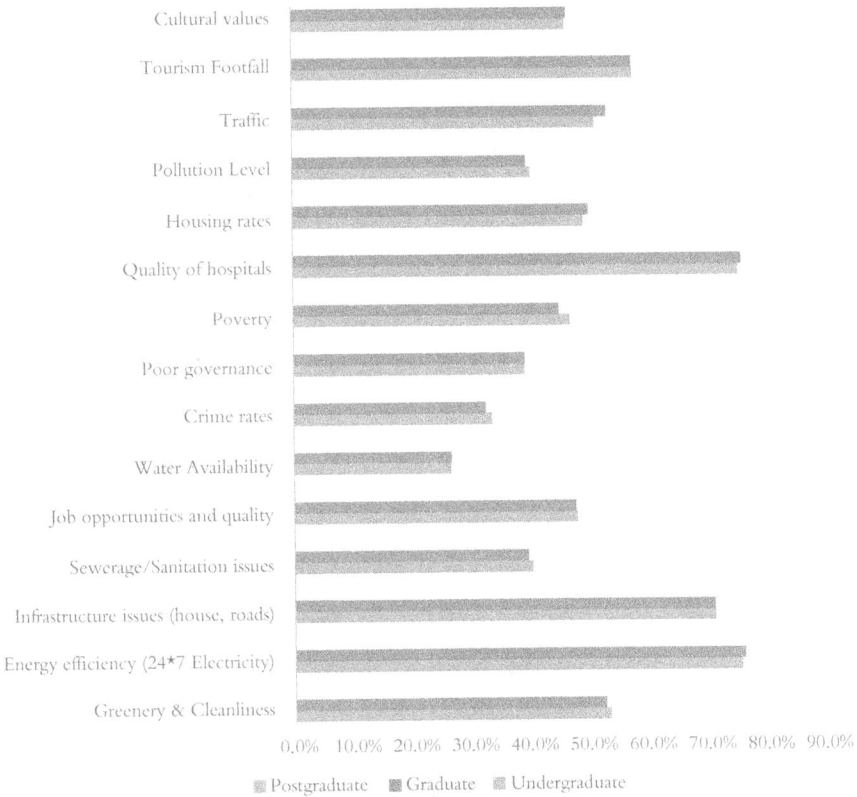

Figure 7.17: Perceived improvement of challenges in the next five years

7.15 Prioritization of Issues

The respondents have expressed their views about prioritization of features in making their city into a smart city. Figure 7.18 shows that the there is no significant difference in perceptions of all education groups. For all the education groups, more than (50%) of respondents shared that for the civic bodies, safety and security, water management, sanitation, energy efficiency, air quality, waste water management, water supply, energy supply, education, health, economy and employment should be given highest priorities.

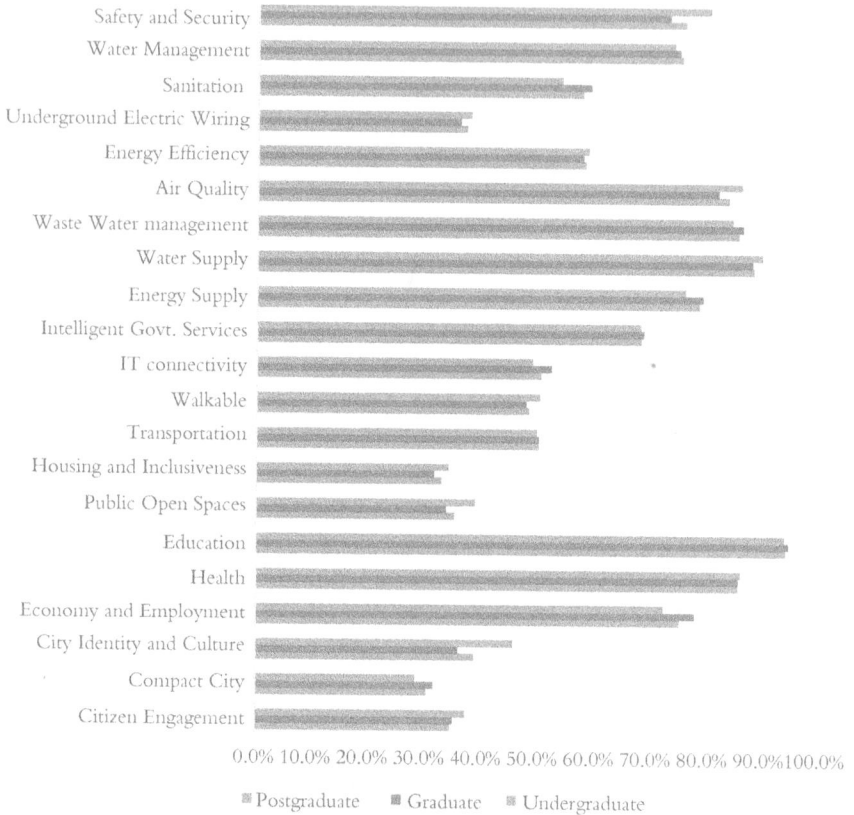

Figure 7.18: Prioritization of Issues

Chapter 8
Youth Engagement Outcomes and Recommendations

- The study has found that the ideas from young minds are very important to make a smart city. The priorities in a smart city are smart governance, health facilities, houses, education and employment, smart infrastructure, a clean and green environment. It is concluded that the respondents of different institutions have a good level of knowledge about new technologies and smart cities.

- Respondents prioritize house, employment, education for all in the first place and medical facilities are their second choice. Likewise, (20.8%) respondents prioritize smart and effective governance and citizen engagement, (17%) have priorities set on clean and green city and (14.9%) on developing into a world class city consisting of smart and efficient services.

- The study indicates that the major challenges are – increasing traffic, decline in greenery and cleanliness, increasing housing rates, poor governance, low job opportunities and quality, increasing crime rates, poverty and water problem. Based on the study analyses, it is evident that respondents are still facing a dearth of basic facilities and Delhi needs to address these challenges at different levels.

- The perceived improvement in challenges in the next five years is maintaining greenery and cleanliness, energy efficiency, traffic, increasing housing rate, poor governance, job opportunities and quality, increasing crime problem, sewerage/sanitation issues, pollution level and poverty and water availability. Similarly, there are other challenges as well which are perceived as potential areas of improvement in the next five years.

- As a means of transport respondents have preferred metro followed by bus, auto and car for five days in week. Very few said that they do not use metro, bus or auto in their everyday journey and depend on personal car or scooter.

- Out of the total respondents, (34.2%) said that they take less than 30 minutes to travel to their workplace. About (36.2%) of respondents need between 30 minutes to one hour, (27.5%) between one to two hours and a few replied more than two hours. The data says that the majority of respondents reside near their workplace and do not need to travel a lot to reach their destination or university.

- (43.7%) of respondents said that that they spend an amount between ₹1001 – ₹3000 monthly for commuting. (25.7%) said that they spend less than ₹1000 per month. (15%) respondents said it costs them ₹3001 – ₹5000 and (15.7%) spend above ₹5000 on transport. The argument here is that many of the respondents belong to middle class/lower middle–class families. They don't want to spend more on travelling and often choose to stay close to their travel destinations.

- (68%) respondents have agreed and (22.7%) strongly agreed that the cost of transport will increase in the future. (7.3%) and (2%) disagree and strongly disagree respectively on the thought of increase in transportation costs. Respondents also replied that the key reasons for increasing mobility costs are hike in price rate of petrol and energy and insufficient public transport. About (38%) respondents have replied that they are satisfied with their monthly expenditure on mobility. (23.1%) said they are neither satisfied nor very satisfied, (21.4%) were dissatisfied. A very few (6%) said they are very dissatisfied with their expenditure on mobility. Here, we can conclude that there is a significant percentage of people who are dissatisfied with their current expenditure on mobility. They urge for the kind of public transport which can save both their time and money.

- Respondents shared that the problem with public transport is related to non-reliability especially during non-peak hours. About (80.3%) said that the waiting period is too long for preferred route. (72.4%) said that there are problems related to safety issues in public buses because they are mostly overcrowded. A significant percentage of respondents also said that last mile connectivity is not available. So, the data represents that there are multiple problems associated with public transportation and there is an urgent need to address these problems by the concerned authorities at different levels.

- When it comes to the question of personal safety during traveling in public transport, (37.5%) said it is average and (26.7%) said it is good. A relatively small percentage (11.5%) of respondents have replied that the safety measures in public transport are very good. About (15.2%) said it is poor and (9.1%) said it is very poor. The study reveals that there are still there requirements of safety measures in public transportation because a significant percentage of people were of the opinion that present safety measures are inadequate and there is a need to develop good transportation facilities especially for women and elderly people.

- Respondents shared that the traffic management will improve to a greater extent. (39.9%) said that parking management will improve, (35.2%) said that there would be an improvement of bicycle rental and mobility infrastructure and (22.2%) think that car share platform will improve. Similarly, (66.8%) respondents have viewed that there would be somewhat improvement on the car share platform, (59.8%) think the same about traceability and logistic applications and (47%) about management of means of transport. This shows that the transport system will become efficient in the coming years.

- The study revealed that there has been less progress on bicycle rental and mobility infrastructure, charging points for electric cars and on parking management. However, the majority of respondents agree that there will be improvement in the area of the car share platform, traceability and logistic applications, traffic management and bicycle rental and mobility infrastructure in the coming years.

- The study revealed that the respondents agree that an efficient public transport system would serve the real purpose of a larger public because a majority of people depend on public transport for their daily travel. The government of Delhi also came up with new plans and strategies to make public transport more convenient. Keeping the fact in mind, government of Delhi emphasized improving public transport as it is considered to be the better mode of travel for larger population.

- The study shows that metro is the best option for the majority of the respondents. (54.4%) of viewers have said that the metro is the most convenient and available transport in Delhi. (24.8%) viewers have stated that there would be improvement of road conditions. (13.5%) of respondents have expressed that prefer metro over buses, but buses are a secondary option.

- The study reveals that metro is a better choice than other means of transportations for the majority of respondents. The respondents shared that metro helps them avoid traffic and enables them to reach them their work places in stipulated time period as compared to buses and other private transports.

- Out of total respondents, (40.8%) said that they are able to pay less than ₹1000 per month as many of them belong to the middle–class and they do not have other sources of income to support their study. (37.2%) replied that they are able to pay between ₹1001 – ₹3000 for travelling in their everyday life. (12.3%) said it is between ₹3001 – ₹5000 and (9.7%) said that they can spend more than ₹5000 on public transport. Here, the study reveals that the majority of respondents can spend between ₹1001 – ₹3000 on public transport and a few said they can afford more than ₹3001 – ₹5000 per month. So, the public transport in a smart city has to be cheap and affordable.

- The data highlights that (89.1%) of respondents give more priority to building road networks to support green transport, followed by (87.2%) who think that developing infrastructural support by installing charging stations is important, (87.0%) on ensuring a sufficient supply of electricity for each family and (82.6%) on providing subsidy to manufacturers. The data also show that (54.2%) respondents support providing subsidies to consumers, which is a secondary priority in comparison to others. It can be concluded from the study that Delhi needs to build road networks, infrastructure support and supply of sufficient electricity for each family in order to support the green transport system which is crucial for a future smart city.

- The study reveals that measures like restricting the use of pollution causing vehicles and fuels, promoting car sharing, enhancing transport coordination through real-time updates, improving the efficiency of bus transport operation, encouraging green modes/transports and compliance for vehicle emission standards and inspection and maintenance have to be taken into consideration by the government seriously in order to visualize a global smart city.

- The data shows only one-fourth of the respondent agree that the mobility of foods and vegetables is very efficient, but there is a significant percentage of people who have agreed that the mobility of goods in Delhi is efficient.

- When it comes to the question of average performance, respondents shared that removal of electronic waste, construction/demolition waste, medical/clinical waste is average in Delhi.

- It can be derived from the study that the transport system for removal of waste material is better in the areas of removal of electronic waste and agricultural waste in comparison to other categories.

Findings from Cross Tabulation Observations

8.1.1. *Analysis of perceptions by surveyed cities*

- The study reveals that respondents have said that the major challenges in Delhi are increasing traffic, rise in pollution, decline in greenery and cleanliness, increasing housing rate, poor governance, low job opportunities and quality, increasing crime problem, poverty and water problem.
- The respondents of Gurugram also face a lot of challenges. The major problems include a decline in greenery & cleanliness, poverty, increasing traffic, rise in pollution, low job opportunities and job quality and increasing crime rates.
- Similarly, the challenges in Lucknow include increasing traffic, rise in pollution, decline in greenery and cleanliness, drop in cultural values, poor governance, sewerage/sanitation issues, job opportunities and quality, increasing crime problem, infrastructure issues followed by other challenges like job opportunities and job quality and infrastructure issues.
- The study revealed that respondents are still facing lack of basic facilities and all cities need to address these challenges at different levels. The respondents in Noida have expressed that the major challenges are increased traffic and rise in pollution.

- The perceived improvement of challenges in the next five years in Delhi include greenery and cleanliness, energy efficiency, increasing traffic, poverty and job opportunities. The data also shows that according to the respondents there will be a decrease in infrastructure issues, crime rates, traffic and tourism footfall, poor governance. Respondents also expressed that water availability and housing rate will get worse.

- In Gurugram, respondents have said there will be an improvement in greenery and cleanliness, energy supply, poverty and pollution level. The respondents also expressed that there will be a decrease in areas of infrastructure, crime rate and tourism footfall. A small percentage of respondents have said that things will get worse in the future. However, there are some areas which need to be addressed such as water availability and traffic. In Lucknow, respondents have expressed that there will be an improvement in areas of greenery and cleanliness, energy efficiency, infrastructure, sewerage/sanitation, job opportunities and quality of hospitals. The data indicates that there will be a decrease in the areas of crime rates, poverty and traffic. The respondents have also said that the areas of greenery, cleanliness and energy supply will get worse.

- Respondents in Noida shared that the major areas that will improve across the cities include cleanliness and greenery, energy efficiency, infrastructure, sewerage/sanitation, traffic, crime rates which need to be addressed by the concerned authorities.

- The respondents have shared that the high prioritized areas in all the cities include health facilities, education, water supply, energy supply, safety and security, waste water management and air quality. The study highlights that there are many challenges faced by respondents of Lucknow but the major ones are safety, security and air quality.

- The study highlights that in Delhi, (17.4%) of respondents spend an amount between ₹3001 – ₹5000 per month for commuting. (48.4%) spend between ₹1001 – ₹3000 per month and (22.6%) spend less than ₹1000 per month. A significant percentage of respondents (11.5%) spend above ₹5000 a month. The argument here is that many respondents included in the study are unemployed and belong to middle class/lower middle-class families. They do not want to spend more on traveling and often choose to stay at places near to their travel destination.

- Similarly, in Gurugram, (17%) of respondents have said that they spend amount between ₹3001 – ₹5000 for commuting. (48%) said they spend between ₹1001 – ₹3000. Around (23%) spend less than ₹1000 rupee per month.

- In Noida, (16%) of respondents have stated that they spend an amount between ₹3001 – ₹5000, (46.3%) spend between ₹1001 – ₹3000 and (22.9%) spend less than ₹1000 per month. In Lucknow, the scenario is a bit different than Delhi and Gurugram. In Lucknow, (29.8%) of respondents have stated that they spend above ₹5000 per month. Approximately (36.9%) spend less than ₹1000 and only (6.7%) between ₹3001– ₹5000.

- Respondents across regions highlighted that the key reasons in increasing mobility cost are hike in prices of petrol and energy in all cities. Insufficient public transport and availability are also reasons for increase in mobility costs in the future.

- In Delhi, (68.6%) respondents agree that the cost will increase in the future, (23.9%) strongly agreed with this while (6.0%) and (1.5%) respectively said that they disagree and strongly disagree with it. In Gurugram, (69.2%) respondents agree with the increase in traveling cost, (24.2%) strongly agree and (5.4%) of respondents disagree with this perception. In Noida, (66.9%) respondents agree with the increase in expenditure. (25.7%) strongly agree (4.6%) respondents disagree and (2.9%) strongly disagree with the statement. Similarly, in Lucknow (66.3%) respondent agree with the increase in commuting expenditures, (16.9%) strongly agree, (13.4%) disagree and (3.5%) strongly disagree.

- The data highlights that there is a significant percentage of people who are dissatisfied with their current expenditure on mobility. They urge for the kind of public transport which can save both their time and money.

- Out of the total respondents in Delhi, (95.6%) said that the problem is related to waiting period, which is too long for preferred route. (93.2%) think that non-reliability of public transport especially during non-peak hours is the major problem and (85.6%) think that public transport is not safe for belongings and an equal percentage of people also think that non–availability at last mile connectivity is also a major problem. About (78.3%) of respondents have viewed that the vehicles are generally overcrowded.

- In Gurugram, (100%) of the respondents have said that the major problem is related to waiting period which is too long for preferred route. (97.3%) people believe non-reliability, especially during non-peak hours, is a big problem. (88.5%) think that last mile connectivity is not available, (87.3%) feel that their belongings are not safe in public transports and (74.6%) said that the vehicles are generally overcrowded.

- In Noida, (100%) of the respondents view waiting period as a major issue which is too long for preferred route. (97.7%) shared that non-reliability, especially during non-peak hours, is major issue. (87.3%) shared that safety of belongings is a major issue and (83.4%) shared that the vehicles are generally overcrowded.

- In Lucknow, (49.6%) of respondent feel that the major problem is related to overcrowded public transport. (29.8%) think non-reliability, especially during non-peak hours, is the major problem and (19.9%) feel that safety of belongings in public transport is the major issue.

- In Delhi, (12.7%) respondents have replied that the safety measures in public transport are very good, (29.2%) replied it is good, about (39.5%) said its average and (14.1%) said it is poor. The study reveals that there is still a requirement of safety measures in public transportation because a significant percentage of respondents have viewed the present safety measures as inadequate and they feel the need for public transport to be more developed especially for women and elderly people.

- In Gurugram, (13.1%) respondents have stated that the safety measures in public transport is very good, (30.8%) replied good, 38.5% think it's average and (14.6%) said it's poor. In Noida, 12.6% respondents have viewed the safety measures in public transport as very good, (26.3%) replied its average, (41.7%) good and (13.7%) said it is poor.

- In Lucknow, (6.4%) respondents have viewed the safety measures in public transport as very good, (17.3%) replied its average, (29.7%) good and (19.6%) said it is poor. (26.8%) of respondents from Lucknow shared that personal safety is very poor.
- Majority of the respondents have agreed that there will be an improvement in the area of car share platform, traceability and logistic applications, traffic management, bicycle rental and mobility infrastructure.
- More than (50%) of respondents in all surveyed cities shared that mass rapid transit system like metro is going to be the best mode of transport. Here, respondents have viewed that the metro helps them to avoid traffic and makes it possible for them to reach their work places in the stipulated time as compared to buses and other private transport.
- The data shows that there is no significant difference between perceptions of respondents from Delhi, Gurugram and Noida. However, the respondents from Lucknow are not willing to spend amount between ₹3001 – ₹5000 on mobility.
- There are (45.9%) of the respondents from Lucknow who are willing to spend an additional amount of ₹1001 – ₹3000 and (17.3%) of the respondents from the same city can spend an amount of ₹5000 a month.
- In Delhi, (100%) of respondents shared that policies for green transport can be supported by building road networks, (98.6%) of respondents emphasized on providing subsidies to manufacturers, (97.9%) on ensuring sufficient supply of electricity for each family and (97%) viewers have agreed on infrastructural support by installing charging stations.

- In Gurugram, (100%) of respondents have stated that policies for green transport can be supported by building road networks and providing infrastructural support by installing charging stations, (98.6%) think that it can be done by providing subsidies to manufacturers and (99.6%) think it can be done by ensuring sufficient supply of electricity for each family.

- In Noida, (100%) of respondents have expressed that policies for green transport can be supported by building road networks, an equal percent of people support providing subsidies to manufacturers, infrastructural support by installing charging stations and (99.4%) think it can be done by ensuring sufficient supply of electricity for each family.

- Similarly, in Lucknow, (47.1%) of respondents shared that policies for green transport can be supported by building road networks, (46.4%) emphasize on infrastructural support by installing charging stations, (42.9%) support ensuring sufficient supply of electricity for each family and (29.8%) emphasized on by providing subsidies to consumers.

- The respondents also expressed that there has been an increase in population in urban areas in the last two decades and facilities available are not able to meet the needs of the people. So, in order to provide a good transport system, the government has to take all the initiatives that promote the public transport system.

- Respondents have replied that the key reasons behind the increase in commuting expenditure will be a hike in the price rate of petrol and energy in all cities. Insufficient public transport and shortage of availability are some other reasons for increase in mobility cost in future.

- The study revealed that there are multiple problems associated with public transportation in all surveyed cities and there is an urgent need to address these problems by concerned authorities at different levels.
- In Gurugram, (15.2%) respondents think that safety measures in public transport are very good and (15.3%) said it is good. About (13%) said it's average and (8.1%) said it is poor.
- It was concluded from the data that the majority of respondents from all regions have agreed that there will be an improvement in areas of car share platform, traceability and logistic applications, traffic management, bicycle rental and mobility infrastructure.
- The study reveals that in Delhi and Gurugram, buses and metro are preferred choice rather than other means of transport for the majority of respondents. Here, the respondents have viewed that the metro helps them to avoid traffic and enables them to reach their work place in time compared to buses and other private transport.
- Respondents from all the regions have supported measures like restraining the use of polluting vehicles and fuels, promoting car sharing, enhancing transport coordination through real time updates, improving the efficiency of bus transport operation, encouraging green modes/transports, compliance for vehicle emission standards, inspection and maintenance to be taken into consideration by the government seriously in order to visualize a global smart city.
- The study revealed that the transport system for removal of electronic waste and agricultural waste is better than the others.

- In all regions, the transport system to remove construction/demolition waste and industrial waste is extremely inefficient.

8.1.2. *Analysis of perceptions by Gender*

- The data shows that responses from male respondents and female respondents are vary significantly in terms of short-term vision and long-term vision of their city.
- The study revealed that the major challenges faced by male respondents are increasing traffic and rise in pollution, while the major challenges for female respondents are increasing crime rate and sanitation problem.
- The data shows that the perceived improvement of challenges in the next five years as per male respondents are greenery and cleanliness, energy efficiency, poverty, traffic and tourism footfall.
- Similarly, male respondents have also viewed that there will be a decline in infrastructure issues (house, roads) job opportunities and quality and tourism footfall. The areas which will get worse as per the views of male respondent are water availability and housing rates.
- As far the views of female respondents are concerned, the major perceived improvement of challenges in the next five years include energy efficiency (24*7 Electricity), poverty and quality of hospital and tourism footfall. They have also viewed that there will be a decrease in the area of crime rates, job opportunities and quality and traffic. The areas which will get worse as per the views of female respondents include water availability, housing rates and pollution level.

- Male respondents have shared that the high prioritized areas in upcoming smart cities are health, education, water supply, energy supply, safety and security, waste water management and air quality. The medium prioritized areas include housing and inclusiveness, underground electric wiring, sanitation, walkable localities, energy efficiency. Similarly, low priority areas for male respondents are IT connectivity, open public spaces and underground electric wiring.
- According to the female respondents, the high prioritized areas are education, safety and security, water supply, health, water management, economy and employment, energy supply, air quality and waste water management. The medium prioritized areas include housing and inclusiveness, open public spaces, compact city, walkable localities and transportation. As per the views of female respondents the low prioritized areas are open public spaces, compact city and citizen engagement.
- The study revealed that in all cases the majority of male respondents use metro, bus, e-rickshaw and auto for their daily mobility. Very few said that they don't use metro, bus or auto for their daily journey and depend on their personal car or scooter.
- The majority of female respondents use auto, shared auto, scooter and bus in their daily journey within the city.
- Both male and female respondents have also expressed that insufficient public transport facility is one of the key reasons for using personal transport resulting into increased cost of mobility.

- The study revealed that there is a significant percentage of male respondents who are dissatisfied with their current expenditure on mobility as compared to female respondents.
- The major problems for both male and female respondents are waiting period which is too long for preferred route and non-reliability especially during non-peak hours for public transport.
- It can be derived from the study that personal safety during travelling for women is a concern as many of them said that the current facilities of public transport are poor and inadequate. The data indicates that steps should be taken to develop more facilities in public transport, especially for women and elderly people.
- Majority of male and female respondents have agreed that there will be improvement in services of car share platform, traceability and logistic applications, traffic management and bicycle rental and mobility infrastructure.
- In order to meet the needs of people the state governments should emphasize more on public transport as it covers larger population who basically belong to middle or lower income groups. The government should also come up with new plans and strategies to make public transport more convenient.
- The study reveals that for male respondents, buses are the best choice over other means of transportations and for females, private autos and metro is primary choice rather than buses.
- (34.9%) male respondents strongly agree that more than half of the vehicles in India will be replaced by

electric vehicles in 20 years as compared to (47.1%) of female respondents.

8.1.3. *Analysis of perceptions by Income group*

- Respondents shared the information regarding time taken to commute to work or university. The data revealed that there are significant differences in travel pattern up to two hours among all income groups except those who travel more than two hours in a day.
- Two-third of respondents who are in an income group of ₹1 lakh to ₹3 lakh shared that the cost of mobility is between ₹1001-₹3000 through public transport.
- Half of the respondents from the same income group shared that the cost of mobility is between ₹1001 – ₹3000. Not a significant number (less than 20%) from all income groups shared that the cost of mobility is above 5000.
- More than (90%) of the respondents from the all income groups either strongly agree or agree that cost of mobility is going to increase in the coming years.
- All the respondents from all income groups shared that waiting period is too long for the preferred route in public transport. This is for Delhi-NCR and Lucknow and prevents them from relying on public transport modes.
- The data also highlights that more than (95%) of respondents from all income groups found that the public transport modes are not reliable especially during non-peak hours.
- The data revealed that not even a single respondent from any of the income groups feels safe in public transport. More than (40%) of respondents find personal safety

average in public transport. This is alarming and limits the daily commuters that use public transport.

- The data highlights the views of respondents on the services that will improve in the next five years. There are several issues categorically mentioned here and each issue has its own significance for providing better transport system to respondents.
- Respondents shared that parking management, traffic management and management of means of transport is going to be improved in the next five years.
- Respondents from all income groups shared that public transport and shared transport services are likely to be increased in the near future. The percentage of respondents who shared that services for private transport are going to improve is less than (20%) among all age groups.
- When it comes to what is expected to be better for public transport, the study shows that metro is the best option for majority of respondents from all income groups.
- More than (60%) of the respondents whose yearly income is between ₹5 lakh – ₹12 lakh and above ₹12 lakh shared that in terms of public transport modes, trains like metro are going to be increased in the next five years.
- The data revealed that the percentage of respondents who are willing to pay more than ₹5000 is actually less than (12%) among all groups irrespective of their income levels.
- The data revealed that more than (50%) of respondents from all income groups has given more priority to building road networks to support the green transport,

infrastructural support by installing charging stations and ensuring sufficient supply of electricity for each family. The data also revealed that subsidies to the manufacturers is also not significantly endorsed by respondents.

- More than (60%) of respondents from all income groups shared that measures to improve urban transport system can be done through restraining the use of polluting vehicles and fuels.

- More than (50%) of respondents from all the income group shared that the urban transport system can be made more efficient through compliance for vehicle emission standards and inspection & maintenance and through encouraging green modes/transports.

- Close to (70%) of respondents from the income group of less than ₹1 lakh agreed with the statement that more than half of the vehicles in India will be replaced by electric vehicles in 20 years. (60%) from the same income group felt that there will be a fall in green transport prices in the near future. They also feel that an automobile is a necessity for them and represents status in society, such a percentage is more than (60%) in the income group of less than ₹1 lakh.

- A significant percentage of respondents (greater than (50%) in the income group of ₹5 lakh to above ₹12 lakh consider the transport system of food items as efficient.

- A significant number of respondents shared that the efficiency related to mobility of goods such as packers and movers, water supply, fruits and vegetables and manufactured goods is efficient but there is still a requirement to make them more efficient.

- The data highlights the perceptions about transport system for removal of waste material which is not efficient in Delhi–NCR and Lucknow.
- More than (50%) of respondents from the income group of less than ₹1 lakh shared that transport system for removal of waste material such as construction/demolition waste, industrial waste and municipal waste is not efficient in the city.
- The data revealed that more than (50%) of the respondents are facing challenges in infrastructure related issues, sewerage/sanitation related issues, job opportunities and their quality, increased crime rates, poor governance, increased poverty, lack of quality of hospitals, sudden rise in pollution and increased traffic.
- The data revealed that education, health, waste water management, air quality, water management, economy and employment are more important in all income groups.

8.1.4. Analysis of perceptions by Education Group

- Respondents shared the information regarding time taken to commute to work or university. The data revealed that there is no significant difference in travel pattern up to two hours among the all education groups.
- All respondents from all education groups shared that waiting period is too long for the preferred route in public transport. This is for Delhi–NCR and Lucknow and prevents them from relying on public transport modes.
- The data also highlights that more than (80%) of the respondents from all education groups found that public

transport modes are not reliable especially during non-peak hours.

- The data revealed that not even a single respondent from any of the education groups feels safe in public transport. More than (40%) of respondents find personal safety average in public transport. This is alarming and prevents daily commuters from using public transport.

- The data highlights the views of respondents on services that will improve in the next five years. There are several issues categorically mentioned here and each issue has its own significance for providing better transport system to the society.

- Respondents shared that parking management, traffic management and management of means of transport is going to improve in the next five years.

- Respondents from all the age groups shared that public transport and shared transport services are likely to increase in the near future.

- The percentage of respondents who shared that the services for private transport are going to be improved is less than (20%) among all the age groups.

- When it comes to what is expected to be better for public transport, the study shows that metro is the best option for majority of respondents from all education groups.

- More than (50%) of respondents from all education groups shared that in terms of public transport mode, trains like metro are going to increase in the next five years.

- The data revealed that the percentage of respondents who are willing to pay more than ₹5000 is actually less than (10%) irrespective of their education levels.
- The data revealed that more than (60%) of respondents from all education groups have given more priority to building road networks to support green transport, infrastructural support by installing charging stations and ensuring sufficient supply of electricity for each family.
- More than (60%) of respondents from all education groups shared that one of the measures to improve the urban transport system is restraining the use of polluting vehicles and fuels.
- More than (50%) of respondents from all education groups shared that urban transport systems can be made more effecient through compliance for vehicle emission standards and inspection & maintenance and through encouraging green modes/transports.
- Close to (35%) of respondents from all education groups agreed with the statement that more than half of the vehicles in India will be replaced by electric vehicles in 20 years. Less than (20%) from all the education groups feel that there will be a fall in green transport prices in the near future.
- Only less than (10%) of students from all education groups believe that green transport is expensive. It can be concluded that education does not contribute to a significant difference among youth perceptions.
- It was observed that the perception of those respondents who had completed their graduation degree is marginally higher among other education groups.

- More than (20%) of respondents from all education groups shared that transport system for removal of waste material such as construction/demolition waste, industrial waste and municipal waste is not efficient in the city.
- The data revealed that more than (40%) of respondents are facing challenges in infrastructure related issues, sewerage/sanitation related issues, job opportunities and their quality, increased crime rates, poor governance, increased poverty, lack of quality of hospitals, sudden rise in pollution and increased traffic. This shows that respondents are facing many more issues in their life and traffic congestion and modes of transport is one of the issues.
- It can be concluded that there is no significant difference in perceptions of all education groups.

8.2 Recommendations

8.2.1 Recommendations for smart transport

Transport Issues
- Widening of roads, building walk-over bridges for pedestrians and building a circle road around key areas are some solutions to traffic problems.
- Multi-level parking facilities should be implemented.
- Technology should be used to provide better parking and transportation solutions.
- Flyovers should be constructed at strategic places.
- Dedicated bicycle and walking lanes should be present, bicycle sharing should be facilitated.
- Services provided by public transportation must be improved and their use should be encouraged; it should

reach every corner of the city and should be made economically viable for everyone to use.

Traffic solution and pollution control

- Road conditions should be improved; they should be constructed using good quality material, must be wide and should have visible markings, especially in city outskirts.
- Traffic signals must be followed by citizens and people must be punished if they break traffic rules.
- Bridges and circles must be made at key points where there is more traffic.
- Traffic police must be on roads doing their duty from 8 a.m. to 11 a.m. and from 5 p.m. to 9 p.m.
- CCTV cameras must be installed at various locations to keep an eye on traffic.
- Encourage electric cars through various incentives schemes.

8.2.2 Recommendations for Smart City

Poor Project Execution

- An independent monitoring body should be in place to ensure timely execution of projects.
- Definite deadline should be set and discrepancies should be checked.
- Projects should be privatized for quicker implementation.

Solid Waste Management

- All houses should manage their own waste by generating compost and by deploying dustbins.
- This sector should be privatized including environment-friendly disposal.

- More dumping and recycling centers should be started across the city.

Sewage/Wastewater/Drainage

- Modernizing of the existing system and incorporation of new water-saving techniques should be implemented.
- Integrated sewage plan for the entire city should be made; adding new sewage plants in line with city topography.
- Sensor alarms should be installed for any kind of leakage.

Unemployment

- More jobs should be created in industrial, commercial and IT space.
- Being centrally located, development of cities from the perspective of logistics is possible.
- Tourist attraction will generate more employment opportunities.
- Initiatives and schemes should be undertaken to employ and retain the digitally literate and talented youth that pass out of several degree-level colleges in Delhi and surrounding cities.

Civic Responsibility

- Strict laws should be implemented and monitored to ensure compliance.
- Awareness of laws and penalties for negligence is a must.

Provide Employment to Large numbers

- Delhi-NCR may be projected as a start-up hub and service providers can be encouraged to set up their offices. In doing so, Delhi-NCR and Lucknow would attract talent from other states.

- Delhi-NCR should use its advantage of strategic location and should convert itself as a logistic hub.
- It should focus more on tourism; this will provide new job opportunities.
- Entrepreneurship must be encouraged.

Better Sewerage, Sanitation and Waste Management

- Proper sanitation facilities must be provided to all citizens in slums, awareness about the use of toilets spread and open-defecation discouraged.
- The government should build more public toilets in slum areas.
- Respondents feel that very few initiatives have been launched for rain-water harvesting and other techniques of saving water like installing water meters to detect and prevent leakages in pipes. Hence, proper techniques should also be implemented in these areas.
- A proper mechanism for treating all waste water in the city must be incorporated which will enable reuse of water for secondary purposes.

Provide affordable Transport mode

- The respondents of Delhi-NCR and Lucknow feel that the current public transport system is a big challenge.
- A lot of colleges are on the outskirts of Delhi-NCR and Lucknow where public transport is not accessible round the clock.
- Auto rickshaws in surveyed cities (especially in Gurugram, Noida and Lucknow) do not travel by

meter, which is a burden to respondents, as they end up paying much more than a meter would have charged them.

- Frequency and service of existing public transport for the preferred bus route is very poor and needs improvement.
- Hence, the respondents want a more integrated and reliable transport system in Delhi–NCR and Lucknow, which would result in better productivity over time for all.

Glossary

Youth Engagement	Taking opinions from youth for making plans/strategies for betterment of the city.
Identity and culture	Each city has a unique identity, which distinguishes it from all other cities, like location or climate, industry, cultural heritage, local culture, etc.
Economy and employment	Robust and resilient economic base and growth strategy that creates large scale employment and increased opportunities for majority of its citizens.
Health	Access to healthcare for all its citizens.
Education	Education opportunities for all children in the city.
Mixed use	Different kind of land uses in same places, such as offices, housing, shops clustered together.
Compactness	Place of stay and work are close to public transport.
Open spaces	Sufficient and usable open spaces are mostly green and used for exercise and outdoor recreation by all age groups. Access to all people.
Housing and inclusiveness	Housing for all income groups and integration among social groups.

Transportation and Mobility	Minimum requirement of transport to move around, good public and private transport modes.
Walkable localities	Reduce congestion, air pollution and resource depletion, boost local economy, promote interactions and ensure security. The road network is created or refurbished not only for vehicles and public transport, but also for pedestrians and cyclists and necessary administrative services are offered within walking or cycling distance.
IT connectivity	Robust internet network allowing high-speed connections to all offices and houses.
Intelligent government services	Easy interaction between citizen and government, via online and telephonic services.
Energy supply	24★7 electricity supply, no delays in repairs.
Energy source	At least 10% of electricity generated by renewables.
Water supply	24★7 good quality water supply.
Waste water management	Advance water management programs which include smart meters, rain water harvesting and green infrastructure to manage storm water runoffs.
Water quality	Take care of sewage to prevent water from polluting, thereby ensuring good water quality.

Air quality	Ensure good quality air by reducing pollution by various methods.
Energy efficiency	Use of energy efficiency practices in buildings, street lights and transit systems.
Underground electric wiring	Use of underground electric wiring to avoid black outs due to storm and to eliminate unsightliness.
Sanitation	No open defecation and a full supply of toilets for all citizens.
Waste management	Waste management system which removes household and commercial garbage and disposes it environmentally and economically.
Safety	Safety for all people and especially women and children, at all times.

As you all know, the Indian government is taking major steps to transform its cities into modern & sustainable habitation for providing better quality of life. To meet future challenges in areas of mobility, infrastructure, water and waste treatment, greening of cities, better governance and other resources some 100 cities have been selected.

You all are current and future users of these cities and the current work will identify provisions, which are important to young people like you and how these priorities change with your needs with time. Additionally, we are studying the aspects of mobility in detail considering usage of private vehicles, public transport, time spent and its main bottlenecks. We also want to know your expectations from the government and amount of money you are willing to pay extra for better services.

This work will inform government, policy makers, industries, society and developers of smart cities to help them plan resources towards providing such provisions in smart cities. This work will be useful in developing public debate on issues – both, focussing on public and private resources to solve identified problems in smart cities and change in young persons' behaviours to contribute to sustainable smart cities. An example of such behaviour will be modal shift from privately owned vehicles to more efficient public transport.

If you don't want to participate in the survey, you are free to leave. Only those interested in participating in the survey need to complete the questionnaire. If you don't want to answer any question, you may leave it blank or you may leave in the middle of completing the questionnaire as well- the questionnaire will be destroyed.

If you feel uncomfortable during the survey please let us know and we will provide you with assistance.

We thank you for your time and inputs in this important study.

Questionnaire

Gender

☐ **Male**   ☐ **Female**

Age _____ **City Name** _____
Area (Urban/Rural) _____

1. **What is the area of study you are enrolled in or completed?**
   1. Commerce
   2. Communication
   3. Computer Science/ IT
   4. Design
   5. Economics
   6. Education
   7. Engineering
   8. Environment
   9. Fashion
   10. Arts
   11. Finance
   12. Law
   13. Management
   14. Neuropsychology & Neurosciences
   15. Real Estate And Urban Infrastructure
   16. Sanskrit Studies
   17. Social Science
   18. Travel & Tourism
   19. Other

2. **Current Education Level**
   ☐ Under Graduate   ☐ Master's
   ☐ Graduate   ☐ Higher Studies (M. Phil, Ph.d)

3. Number of family members
a) Upto 2   b) 3-5   c) More than 5

4. What is your family income (Yearly in ₹)?
☐ Nil
☐ 1,00,000 – 3,00,000
☐ 3,00,001 – 5,00,000
☐ 5,00,001 – 8,00,000
☐ 8,00,001 – 12,00,000
☐ Above 12,00,000

5. Type of residence
☐ Own
☐ Rented

6. Elements for City Vision (please rank these from 1 – highest to 6 – lowest)

Short term (with respect to five years)		Long Term (with respect to 10-20 years)	
Vision Elements	Rank	Vision Elements	Rank
Clean and Green City		Clean and Green city	
Smart Infrastructure		Develop into world class city consisting of smart and efficient services	
Houses, Employment and Education for all		House, employment, education for all	
Smart Governance		Good medical facilities	
Health facilities for all		Smart and effective governance and citizen engagement	
Other 1		Other 1	

7. Current Challenges Faced by Citizens (Multiple options allowed)

Challenges area	Yes / No	Challenges area	Yes / No
Decline in Greenery & Cleanliness		Poverty	
Energy efficiency (24★7 Electricity)		Lack of Quality of hospitals	
Infrastructure issues (house, roads)		Increasing housing rates	
Sewerage/Sanitation issues		Rise in pollution	
Job opportunities and quality		Increased Traffic	
Water problems		Fall/drop in tourism	
Increased crime rates		Drop in Cultural values	
Poor governance			

8. Perceived Improvement of Challenges in the Next Five Years (Multiple options allowed)

Variables	Will Improve	Wil Decrease	Will get worse
Greenery & Cleanliness			
Energy efficiency (24★7 Electricity)			
Infrastructure issues (house, roads)			
Sewerage/Sanitation issues			

Variables	Will Improve	Wil Decrease	Will get worse
Job opportunities and quality			
Water Availability			
Crime rates			
Poor governance			
Poverty			
Quality of hospitals			
Housing rates			
Pollution Level			
Traffic			
Tourism Footfall			
Cultural values			
Other 1			

9. Prioritization of Features in Making Delhi a Smart City.

Smart City Features	High Priority	Medium Priority	Low Priority	Not at all Important
Citizen Engagement				
Compact City				
City Identity and Culture				
Economy and Employment				
Health				
Education				
Public Open Spaces				

Smart City Features	High Priority	Medium Priority	Low Priority	Not at all Important
Housing and Inclusiveness				
Transportation				
Walkable				
IT connectivity				
Intelligent Govt. Services				
Energy Supply				
Water Supply				
Waste Water management				
Air Quality				
Energy Efficiency				
Underground Electric Wiring				
Sanitation				
Water Management				
Safety and Security				

Preferences for a mobility

10. How frequently do you use public transport?

Transport Type		5+ days a week	2-4 days a week	Once a week	Once a month	More than in a month
Public transport	Bus					
	Metro					

Transport Type		5+ days a week	2-4 days a week	Once a week	Once a month	More than in a month
	Shared Auto					
	E-rick-shaw					
Personal Trans-port	Scooter					
	Car					
	Auto					

11. **How much time does it take you to commute to work / university? (One Side)**
    ☐ Less than 30 minutes
    ☐ Between 30 minutes to 1 hour
    ☐ Between 1 hour to 2 hour
    ☐ More than 2 hour

12. **How much money does it cost? (Per month in ₹)**
    ☐ Less than 1000
    ☐ Between 1001–3000
    ☐ Between 3001–5000
    ☐ Above 5000

13. **Do you think it will increase over time?**
    ☐ Strongly Agree
    ☐ Agree
    ☐ Disagree
    ☐ Strongly Disagree

14. Are you satisfied with this time and money spend?

☐ Very satisfied
☐ Satisfied
☐ Neither
☐ Dissatisfied
☐ Very dissatisfied

15. What problems do you see in public transport? (Check all that apply)

☐ Last mile connectivity is not available
☐ Over – crowded
☐ Not safe for carrying the belongings
☐ Not reliable specially during non-peak hours
☐ Waiting period is too long for preferred route
☐ Any other

16. How would you rate personal safety when travelling by public transport?

☐ Very good   ☐ Poor
☐ Good   ☐ Very Poor
☐ Average

17. What are the services which (you think) will improve in near future?

Variables	To a Great Extent	Some-what	Very Little	Not at All
Car-share platform				
Parking management				
Bicycle rental and mobility infrastructure				

Variables	To a Great Extent	Some-what	Very Little	Not at All
Traffic management (Detector of free parking places)				
Management of means of transport				
Charging points for electric cars				
Traceability and logistics applications				

18. **What is expected to be better in a future smart city?**
    ☐ Public transport   ☐ Shared transport
    ☐ Private transport

19. **What is expected to be better for personal transport?**
    ☐ Buses   ☐ Private Autos
    ☐ Trains like Metro   ☐ Other
    ☐ Good roads

20. **How do you think, government policy can encourage Green Transport (Check all that apply):**
    ☐ By providing subsidy to consumers
    ☐ By providing subsidy to manufacturers
    ☐ Through infrastructural support by installing charging stations
    ☐ By building road network, to support the Green Transport

☐ Ensuring sufficient supply of electricity for each family
☐ None of the above
☐ Any other _____

21. What are the policy measures which could improve urban transport system? (Check all that apply)

☐ Focusing on public transport particularly bus transport
☐ Introducing variety of bus transport services
☐ Improving the efficiency of bus transport operation
☐ Enhancing transport coordination through real time update
☐ Promoting car sharing/pooling
☐ Restraining the use of polluting vehicles and fuels
☐ Compliance for vehicle emission standards and inspection and maintenance
☐ Encouraging green modes/transports
☐ Any other

22. How much additional money will you like pay for a better public transport?

☐ Less than 1000 INR per month
☐ Between 1001–3000 INR per month
☐ Between 3001–5000 INR per month
☐ Above 5000 INR per month

23. This questions deals with various variables related to automobile and green transport. For each of the following statements, please indicate how much you agree or disagree. There is no preferred answer.

Variable	Strongly Agree	Agree	Neutral	Disagree	Strongly Disagree
Using public transportation other than a car helps preserve the environment					
I am currently trying my best to reduce car use					
An automobile is a necessity for me.					
Automobiles represent status in society.					
Public transport is easy to use.					
Green transports are expensive.					
A network of charging facilities is a prerequisite for the use of Green Transport					
There is no need to reduce car use if I use a green transport.					
There will be a fall in green transport prices in the near future.					
More than half of vehicles in India will be replaced by electric vehicle in 20 years					

Questions related to mobility of goods

24. How do you rate the transport system for mobility of the goods?

Particulars	Very efficient	Efficient	Average	Not efficient	Extremely inefficient
Food items					

Particulars	Very efficient	Efficient	Average	Not efficient	Extremely inefficient
Fruits and Vegetables					
Manufac-tured goods					
Construc-tion material					
Supply of water					
Packer and Movers					

25. How do you rate transport system for removal of waste material?

Sources of Waste Material	Very efficient	Efficient	Average	Not efficient	Extremely inefficient
Municipal sources of waste					
Medical/ Clinical sources of waste					
Agricultural sources of waste					
Industrial sources of waste					
Construction/ demolition sources of waste					
Electronic sources of waste					

Name of the Institution_____   Date_____

Bibliography

Banerjee, S. (2017, July 10). *Congestion on Delhi roads has worsened – says new analysis by CSE of latest Google map data.* Retrieved from http://www.cseindia.org: http://www.cseindia.org/congestion-on-delhi-roads-has-worsened--6994

BBA|mantra. (2018). *Project Report: Impact of Lucknow Metro on Transportation System - BBA|mantra. [online] Available at: https://bbamantra.com/project/impact-lucknow-metro-transportation/ [Accessed 12 July. 2018].*

Carlos, F. P. (2010). *Shanghai Manual – A Guide for Sustainable Urban Development in the 21st Century. In SUSTAINABLE URBAN TRANSPORT.* Retrieved from http://www.un.org/esa/dsd/susdevtopics/sdt_pdfs/shanghaimanual/Chapter%204%20-%20Sustainable%20urban%20transport.pdf

Chettri, S. (2017, March 27). *Delhi municipal corporations make classrooms smart, but fail students.* Retrieved from https://www.hindustantimes.com: https://www.hindustantimes.com/delhi-news/delhi-municipal-corporations-make-classrooms-smart-but-fail-students/story-yJGRM72t4FQwx9uvjSQhQM.html

Dave, D. (2016, September 20). *Affordable Transportation Options While Volunteering In Delhi.* Retrieved from https://www.volunteeringindia.com: https://www.volunteeringindia.com/blog/affordable-transportation-options-while-volunteering-in-delhi/

Delhi BRT System – Lessons Learnt. (2016). Retrieved from http://www.dimts.in: http://www.dimts.in/pdf/Delhi_BRT_System_Lessons_Learnt.pdf

Delhi Metro's Cumulative Ridership for the financial year 2016-2017 crosses one billion (100 crores). (2017, March 29th). Retrieved from http://www.delhimetrorail.com: http://www.delhimetrorail.com/press_reldetails.aspx?id=ZlXC4jMrU00lld

Delhi witnesses rapid increase in unemployment. (2017, March 8). Retrieved from http://indianexpress.com/: http://indianexpress.com/article/jobs/delhi-jobs-hiring-recruitment-witnesses-post-graduate-diploma-education-rapid-increase-in-unemployment-4560159/

EcoMobility sessions 2017@COP23. (2017, November 15th). Retrieved from https://ecomobility.org: https://ecomobility.org/wp-content/uploads/2017/11/EcoMobility_COP23-2017-11-10.pdf

Economic Survey of Delhi 2016 - 2017. (n.d.). Retrieved from http://delhi.gov.in: http://delhi.gov.in/wps/wcm/connect/72b434004054dc08bf10ffa1527a7156/Chapter+5.pdf?MOD=AJPERES&lmod=-1210409313&CACHEID=72b434004054dc08bf10ffa1527a7156

Global Greenhouse Gas Emissions Data. (2017, January 19). Retrieved from https://www.epa.gov/ghgemissions/global-greenhouse-gas-emissions-data: https://www.epa.gov/ghgemissions/global-greenhouse-gas-emissions-data

Goswami, S. (2017, November 2). Limit number of e-rickshaws in Delhi to decongest roads, says panel. Retrieved from https://www.hindustantimes.com: https://www.hindustantimes.com/delhi-news/limit-number-of-e-rickshaws-in-delhi-to-decongest-roads-says-panel/story-kTU8AHtnAvOZUHX9imYQmO.htm

http://www.delhimetrorail.com. (2017, March 29th). Retrieved from Delhi Metro's Cumulative Ridership for the financial year 2016-2017 crosses one billion (100 crores): http://www.delhimetrorail.com/press_reldetails.aspx?id=ZlXC4jMrU00lld

http://www.igovernment.in. (2013, Dec 12). Retrieved from Traffic Snarl Snaps 42 Cr Man-Hour From Delhi, NCR Workers:

http://www.igovernment.in/articles/28305/traffic-snarl-snaps-42-cr-man-hour-from-delhi-ncr-workers

https://www.epa.gov/ghgemissions/global-greenhouse-gas-emissions-data. (n.d.). Retrieved from www.epa.gov.

Improving Lives:Urban Infrastrcture. (2017). Retrieved from http://www.makeinindia.com: http://www.makeinindia.com/article/-/v/improving-lives-urban-infrastructure

Issa,Y. (2014, July). Reducing of Roads Congestion Using Demand Management. International Journal of Computational Engineering Research (IJCER), 04(7). Retrieved from http://www.ijceronline.com/papers/Vol4_issue07/Version-2/J0470201020111.pdf

Joseph, H. R., Raina, G., & Jagannathan, K. (2015). Cost estimates for road congestion in Delhi: projections and recommendations. 2015 7th International Conference on Communication Systems and Networks (COMSNETS). Bangalore: IEEE. doi:10.1109/COMSNETS.2015.7098711

(2010). Master Plan for Delhi - 2021. Delhi: Delhi Development Authority. Retrieved from https://dda.org.in/ddanew/pdf/Planning/reprint%20mpd2021.pdf

National Youth Policy 2012. (n.d.). Retrieved from http://www.youthpolicy.org: http://www.youthpolicy.org/national/India_2012_Draft_National_Youth_Policy.pdf

(2013). OECD Regions at a Glance. Paris: Publishing. doi:http://dx.doi.org/10.1787/reg_glance-2013-en

Parashar, B. K. (2018, Feburary 27).To ease traffic jams, Uttar Pradesh may ban e-rickshaws on main routes. Retrieved from https://www.hindustantimes.com: https://www.hindustantimes.com/lucknow/to-ease-traffic-jams-uttar-pradesh-may-ban-e-rickshaws-on-main-routes/story-cLVhTaOUwU8Ow7MfQ5GIOM.html

Planning Commission. (2012). Retrieved from http://12thplan.gov.in/: http://planningcommission.gov.in/plans/planrel/12thplan/welcome.html

Prabhakar, V., Gupta, S., & Mehrotra, R. (2015, September 2). *Smart transportation for Smart Cities.* Retrieved from https://economictimes.indiatimes.com: https://economictimes.indiatimes.com/news/economy/infrastructure/smart-transportation-for-smart-cities/articleshow/48772473.cms

(2013). *Quality of life in cities.* Belgium: Luxembourg. Retrieved from http://ec.europa.eu/regional_policy/sources/docgener/studies/pdf/urban/survey2013_en.pdf

Roy, S. (2017, November 24). *GPS trackers to be installed in all DTC buses.* Retrieved from https://timesofindia.indiatimes.com: https://timesofindia.indiatimes.com/city/delhi/all-dtc-buses-to-get-gps-trackers-soon/articleshow/61774216.cms

Saxena, S. (2011, May 6). *Cluster bus service launched in Delhi.* Retrieved from http://www.thehindu.com: http://www.thehindu.com/todays-paper/tp-national/tp-newdelhi/cluster-bus-service-launched-in-delhi/article1995583.ece

Seetharaman, G. (2015, Dec 12). *City planning and managing public transport are the answers to urban pollution.* Retrieved from https://economictimes.indiatimes.com: https://economictimes.indiatimes.com/news/politics-and-nation/city-planning-and-managing-public-transport-are-the-answers-to-urban-pollution/articleshow/50153478.cms

Singh, R. (2015). *Economic Profile of NCR.* Delhi: National Capital Region Planning. Retrieved from http://ncrpb.nic.in/pdf_files/Final%20Report%20of%20study%20of%20economic%20profile_17122015.pdf

Smart Cities. (2015). Retrieved from http://www.makeinindia.com: http://www.makeinindia.com/article/-/v/internet-of-things

Smart Cities Mission. (2017). Retrieved from http://smartcities.gov.in: http://smartcities.gov.in/content/?cd=OAA3AA%3D%3D

Squires, G. (2012). *Urban and Environmental Economics: An Introduction* (Vol. 1st). Routledge. Retrieved from https://

www.amazon.com/Urban-Environmental-Economics-Graham-Squires/dp/0415619912

Status of Education in Delhi. (2017). Retrieved from http://www. azadindia.org: http://www.azadindia.org/social-issues/status-of-education-in-delhi.html

Strategic Plan of Ministry of Urban Development for 2011-16. (n.d.). Retrieved from http://www.indiaenvironmentportal.org.in: http://www.indiaenvironmentportal.org.in/files/file/Strategic_Plan_draft_new[1].pdf.pdf

The World Factbook. (2017). Retrieved from www.cia.gov/library/ publications/the-world-factbook/fields/2212.html: https://www. cia.gov/library/publications/the-world-factbook/fields/2212. html

Transport System in Delhi. (2018, March 9). Retrieved from http:// www.focusdelhi.com: http://www.focusdelhi.com/infrastructure/ transportation-in-delhi.html

Urban transport Issues for India. (2017). Retrieved from http:// siteresources.worldbank.org: http://siteresources.worldbank. org/INTSARREGTOPTRANSPORT/2045693-1330 028581692/23126045/Prsntn3-Gwilliam.pdf

Weisbrod, G., & Fitzroy, S. (2011). Traffic Congestion Effects on Supply Chains. Croatia: InTech. Retrieved from https:// www.intechopen.com/books/supply-chain-management-new-perspectives/traffic-congestion-effects-on-supply-chains-accounting-for-behavioral-elements-in-planning-and-econo www. worldometers.info. (2018).

Retrieved Jan 2018, 12, from http://www.worldometers.info/world-population/india-population/: http://www.worldometers.info/ world-population/india-population/

www.ingramcontent.com/pod-product-compliance
Lightning Source LLC
Chambersburg PA
CBHW071018280326
41935CB00011B/1402